Romantic comedy is an enduringly popular genre which has maintained its appeal by constantly evolving, from the screwball comedy to the recent emergence of the bromance.

Romantic Comedy examines the history of the genre, considering the social and cultural context for key developments in new genre cycles. It studies the key themes and issues at work within romantic comedy films, focusing in particular on the representation of gender and how the genre acts as a barometer for gender politics in the course of the twentieth century.

Claire Mortimer provides the reader with a comprehensive overview of the genre, tracing its development, enduring appeal, stars and the nature of its comedy. Mortimer discusses both British and Hollywood classic and contemporary romantic comedies, ranging from canonical films to more recent examples which have taken the genre in new directions. In-depth case studies span a wide variety of films, including:

- *It Happened One Night*
- *Bringing Up Baby*
- *Annie Hall*
- *Four Weddings And A Funeral*
- *Bridget Jones's Diary*
- *Wimbledon*
- *Knocked Up*
- *Sex And The City*

This book is the perfect introduction to the romantic comedy genre and will be particularly useful for all those investigating this area within film, media or women's studies.

Claire Mortimer read Film and English Literature at the University of East Anglia. She has worked as a Media and Film Studies teacher for many years, and has been an assistant examiner for Media Studies AS examinations with AQA. She is currently the Head of AS Media Studies and a Lecturer in Film Studies at Colchester Sixth Form College.

Routledge Film Guidebooks

The Routledge Film Guidebooks offer a clear introduction to and overview of the work of key filmmakers, movements or genres. Each guidebook contains an introduction, including a brief history; defining characteristics and major films; a chronology; key debates surrounding the filmmaker, movement or genre; and pivotal scenes, focusing on narrative structure, camera work and production quality.

Bollywood
Tejaswini Ganti

Film Noir
Justus Nieland and Jennifer Fay

James Cameron
Alexandra Keller

Documentary
Dave Saunders

Jane Campion
Deb Verhoeven

Romantic Comedy
Claire Mortimer

Horror
Brigid Cherry

ROMANTIC COMEDY

CLAIRE MORTIMER

Routledge
Taylor & Francis Group

LONDON AND NEW YORK

First published 2010
by Routledge
2 Park Square, Milton Park, Abingdon, Oxon, OX14 4RN

Simultaneously published in the USA and Canada
by Routledge
270 Madison Ave, New York, NY 10016

Routledge is an imprint of the Taylor & Francis Group, an informa business

Typeset in Joanna
by Taylor & Francis Books
Printed and bound in Great Britain by
TJ International Ltd, Padstow, Cornwall

British Library Cataloguing in Publication Data
A catalogue record for this book is available from the British Library

Library of Congress Cataloging in Publication Data
Mortimer, Claire, 1964-
    Romantic comedy / by Claire Mortimer.
        p. cm. – (Routledge film guidebooks)
    Includes bibliographical references and index.
    1. Romantic comedy films–United States–History and criticism. 2.
Romantic comedy films–Great Britain–History and criticism. 3. Love in
motion pictures. I. Title.
    PN1995.9.C55M65 2010
    791.43'617–dc22
                        2009046754

ISBN10: 0-415-54862-4 (hbk)
ISBN10: 0-415-54863-2 (pbk)
ISBN10: 0-203-85143-9 (ebk)

ISBN13: 978-0-415-54862-5 (hbk)
ISBN13: 978-0-415-54863-2 (pbk)
ISBN13: 978-0-203-85143-2 (ebk)

CONTENTS

FIGURES AND TABLES

FIGURES

TABLES

ACKNOWLEDGEMENTS

I would like to thank Sarah Casey for her encouragement, advice and patience during the writing of the book. Many thanks to Aileen Storry and Emily Laughton at Routledge for their hard work and advice. Special thanks to Granville, Arthur and Florence, who have had a lot to put up with.

CREDITS

1

THE ROMANTIC COMEDY

An introduction

Romantic comedy has proved to be one of the most enduring cinematic genres. It has certainly undergone some ebbs and flows in its popularity, but, as with all the major genres, it proves perennially resilient. Audiences still enjoy the blueprint of the romantic comedy, with all its traditional ingredients. Every year sees the release of new romantic comedies, which are strongly in the mould of the earliest examples in cinema history. We want to see the same characters, the same situations, the same narrative trajectory, the same settings and dialogue, with new stars that speak to new generations, yet tell the same story.

The archetypal romantic comedy is certainly perceived to be a woman's film, perhaps dismissed by some, often male, critics and lumped in a category labelled 'chickflick'. Of course, this negative perception of the genre is not just to do with its gendered nature, but has been a fate meted out to genre films in the past. Genre is about mass entertainment, it is about studios maximising their returns on their huge investment in a film, by replicating formulae which have made money in the past. Genre has been seen, in such a context, as anathema to creativity and artistry, and hence critical merit. This attitude seems implicit in the critic Peter Bradshaw's response to *Four Christmases* (2008):

> Vaughan and Witherspoon each demonstrate the classic 'Hollywood romcom' face: waxy as a corpse, dead-eyed with self-loathing, and as smiley and blank as someone who has just consumed their body-weight in Temazepan and Pernod. It has something to do with the way they are lit, or the way they are directed, or with the fact that they have gone into a kind of neuro-physiological shutdown. They know in their hearts that what they are performing is pure ordure …

The film may have merited a poor review, yet the language is permeated with an inherent disdain for the genre. Comedy as a whole has rarely been seen as being as critically respectable as other genres; perhaps it is rather a self-defeating paradox to ask for it to be taken seriously. Even Shakespeare's comedies seem to be critically overshadowed by the tragedies, perhaps diminished by the foregrounding of characters who are not heroic or noble, and themes that concern issues that can be found in everyday life, such as love and relationships, rather than elemental issues of life, death, good and evil. The most respected romcoms are those associated with artistic figures that are respected as auteurs (e.g. Woody Allen's *Annie Hall* and Howard Hawks' *Bringing Up Baby*), lifting them above the negative connotations of the commercial imperative of popular Hollywood cinema.

The essence of genre is the fundamental recipe of repetition and difference. As with all major genres, the romcom blueprint has developed some interesting and successful offshoots, which continue to reinvigorate the form and attract new audiences. These new directions challenge the genre's conventions, stretching the blueprint to its limits, as they borrow and merge with other genres, giving new pleasures to the contemporary audience. This is an audience who are steeped in a heritage of film stretching back over generations. They have ready access to film and media, and welcome the hybridisation of film genres, enjoying the familiar but seeking the new: *Eternal Sunshine of the Spotless Mind*, *Enchanted*, *Knocked Up* and *Shaun of the Dead*.

Tom Ryall comments that 'even the most sharply delineated genres include considerable variety' (1998) and this is certainly true when surveying the breadth of films which are included within the romantic comedy genre. Yet this is ultimately true of all genre films; as Ryall continues, 'this diversity reflects the hybrid generic qualities of many American films and a fluidity of generic boundaries'. This book will consider the films that seem to epitomise the genre conventions that are commonly agreed to be at the heart of the romantic comedy, but will also discuss the films that push the boundaries, that lurk around the periphery of the genre. *Knocked Up*, for example, embraces the humour of gross-out comedy, and hence broadens and renews the appeal of the romcom. In this respect, genre theory can be valuable in serving to expose the 'workings' and generic nature of an individual film, often reminding us that much of Hollywood's product is multigeneric in nature.

As with any genre, certain films have come to be seen as definitive, forming a canon; this delineates the romcom for many, particularly critics and academics. Films such as the classic screwball comedies fall into this category: *Bringing Up Baby, His Girl Friday, The Philadelphia Story*, along with some later landmark romantic comedies including *Annie Hall* and *When Harry Met Sally*. These films are seen to be particularly influential, and tend to dominate discussion of the genre. The canon confers 'classic' status on these films, against which subsequent additions to the genre are compared and often found to be lacking, being dismissed by reviewers as inferior versions of the earlier 'classics'.

DEFINING THE GENRE

What is a romantic comedy? In some respects classifying a film as a romantic comedy can be problematic, as its main elements are present in most films. Romance and comedy, to a greater or lesser extent, can be found in many, or even most, genre films, being a standard source of narrative pleasure. The generation of laughter is the fundamental narrative dynamic within any form of comedy. Nevertheless the narrative can be punctuated by tears and sadness, as the trajectory almost always involves the seeming loss of love and the beloved, when despair and disaster prevail. In this respect the romcom can clearly owe a debt to the romance, featuring a melodramatic tone that can be predominant at certain stages of the narrative. Tamar Jeffers McDonald (2007) observes that the romantic comedy since the late 1980s has placed an emphasis on tears. Suffering is often part of the narrative process of self-discovery and transformation that characterises the genre. *Sex And The City* (2007) sees Carrie go through a process of mourning after Big lets her down on her wedding day. Carrie goes through deep despair and anger, before building her life again, demonstrating strength and resilience. She comes to realise that she was guilty of being selfish, having overlooked Big's needs when planning their wedding, and is then ready to resume their relationship, which we assume to be enhanced by this period of reflection and realisation.

The romcom can be regarded as a hybrid of the romance and comedy genres, featuring a narrative that centres on the progress of a relationship, and, being a comedy, resulting in a happy ending. The dynamic of the film rests on the central quest – the pursuit of love – and almost always leads to a successful resolution.

So what are the elements that compose the genre? A romcom certainly has a very distinctive narrative structure: boy meets girl, various obstacles prevent them from being together, coincidences and complications ensue, ultimately leading to the couple's realisation that they were meant to be together. In keeping with the comedy genre, the narrative concludes with a happy ending, with the final union of the couple. The dominant theme is the 'battle of the sexes', which provides the central dynamic of the genre. The narrative often hinges around the central couple, who initially are antagonistic towards each other, but who come to recognise their inescapable compatibility in the face of great adversity and, often, mutual loathing. Their incompatibility may arise from social status, wealth, conflicting lifestyles and attitudes, or even purely their differing expectations of relationships. The warring couple clearly involves issues regarding gender, as discussed in the chapters on men and women.

Narrative and plot

Stanley Cavell identified a dominant narrative form of the genre which he labelled 'the comedy of remarriage' in his seminal study *Pursuits of Happiness* (1981). This narrative sees the couple as separated in the initial stages, only to be reunited by the end of the film after discovering that they still love each other, as in films such as *His Girl Friday*, *Adam's Rib*, and *Sex And The City*. A second variation on the romcom narrative is that of the couple experiencing love at first sight yet being unable to be together, due to factors beyond their control. Examples of this narrative include *Pretty Woman*, *The Wedding Planner*, and *Enchanted*. A third significant model is that of unrequited love. One half of the couple realises their love for the other early on, but the other half is slow to recognise and return their love, often having to lose the wrong partner in order to be ready for the right love, as in *My Man Godfrey*, *Bringing Up Baby*, and *27 Dresses*. Another identifiable narrative is that of the couple who are at war with each other from the start but come to recognise their love for each other as a result of various misunderstandings and complications. This is a fundamental model for many romantic comedies, as outlined earlier in the chapter. Examples include *It Happened One Night*, *Pillow Talk*, and *How To Lose A Guy In 10 Days*.

All of these variations have a common impetus towards a happy ending. The audience will approach the film in the expectation that the couple will be together, happily, at the end. They can enjoy the journey towards this goal, within the reassurance provided by the very predictability of the plot. The formulaic nature of the genre is often at the heart of the pleasures experienced by the audience.

The narrative will be composed of a sequence of situations that the audience will recognise and, again, expect, from other films of the genre. A typical romantic comedy will feature mistaken identity, disguise and masquerade, intimate tête-à-têtes (often meals), public humiliation, brides bolting from the altar, a race against time, confiding in friends and the 'meet-cute'. The meet-cute is one of the defining moments of the romcom, when the couple first encounter each other, generally in comic and prophetic circumstances. The meet-cute is prophetic in that it can often suggest the nature of the couple's relationship. The situation is used to bring together the two central characters, bringing their conflicting personalities into comic collision, initiating the narrative dynamic. In *Bringing Up Baby* David meets Susan when she commandeers his golf ball, then his car, wrecking his meeting with a potential investor in his museum and damaging his car. Ellie meets Peter in *It Happened One Night* when they fight over the last seat on the bus, Peter pushes himself onto the seat and Ellie ends up, to her fury and embarrassment, on his lap. Both of these examples are typical of the meet-cute involving embarrassment and conflict, but suggesting the future relationship of the couple.

Characters

The central couple are characterised by paradox: they are objects of desire, and yet remain incomplete, and imperfect, until they are ultimately united with each other. Each may offer an image of gender perfection to the audience, often enhanced by the star persona of the actor, and may also be the object of the desire of more than one character, where a 'wrong' partner may be an obstacle in the path to true love. *Pillow Talk* (1959) makes clear how desirable its two lead characters are, as Brad (Rock Hudson) is clearly irresistible to women, whilst Jan (Doris Day) has to fight off the advances of a younger man, resist the proposals of her millionaire client, and becomes the woman for whom the playboy, Brad, overcomes his anti-marriage feelings.

The couple may well demonstrate conflicting character traits, which can help to create initial antagonism that drives the narrative. These traits can prove to be a gift to the other, serving to help them attain greater self knowledge, fulfilment and happiness. On the other hand, one half of the couple may prove themselves to be crippled by need and incompleteness, whether it is the need for love or the need to change, in order to deserve love. In most romcom couples these two states work together, as the narrative shows the couple clashing, and then gradually working through the tumultuous progress of their relationship, until equilibrium is found. *His Girl Friday* revolves around Walter's (Cary Grant) efforts to win back his ex-wife, who is about to remarry. He has already learnt the error of his ways in realising that he *needs* Hildy (Rosalind Russell), as a wife and as a reporter, on his newspaper, whereas Hildy believes that she'll find happiness with the excruciatingly boring insurance salesman, Bruce, as a wife and mother, yet is helpless to resist the attraction of the adventure and excitement that Walter's world offers her.

The film ends with Hildy abandoning the tedium of domestic life for remarriage with Walter and resumption of her career, as her dormant desires and needs are brought back to life via Walter's intervention. The film is typical of the genre in foregrounding the power of love to transform and unite.

Stock characters play a key role in the romcom narrative. Beyond the central couple there may often be other partners, who are rejected in favour of their 'true love'. Best friends will also play a crucial role, being a source of advice, commenting on the relationship, and being a

Figure 1.1 Hildy is in danger of choosing the wrong man in *His Girl Friday*.

repository for the confidences of the couple. The best friend seems very much to be a phenomenon of the romcom since the Woody Allen films of the late 1970s, suggesting the increased emphasis on friendship in filling the void left by fragmented families and communities in the modern world. In this respect it seems significant that friends do not play a significant role in the screwball comedy. The contemporary romantic comedy can surround a central character with a family of friends; Notting Hill and the Bridget Jones films use this device to provide a comic chorus of characters who not only provide a commentary on the central character's love life, but become an extension of their personality and endorse their popularity through the affection they inspire. He's Just Not That Into You takes the theme of friendship as the basis of an ensemble film, featuring a number of rotating narratives regarding relationships which are linked through a network of friends.

The friend can be a foil for the extraordinary characteristics of the central character, serving to accentuate their desirable qualities. Paula (Sarah Jessica Parker) shares her apartment with the intense and quirky Kit (Zooey Deschanel) in Failure To Launch. Kit's response to the mockingbird that keeps her awake at night is to go out and buy a shotgun to get some peace. Kit's brooding unpredictability heightens Paula's image of mature sophistication, which makes her the ideal partner for the playboy, Tripp.

Family can be oddly absent, the characters living in a strange genetic void, as in Sex And The City (2008), where friends are the true family. Family can also be problematic, providing complications and opposition to the relationship. The 2005 romantic comedy Monster-in-Law epitomises this cynicism towards family, as the potential mother-in-law, played by Jane Fonda, does all in her power to prevent the Jennifer Lopez character from marrying her son.

Visual style and iconography

A key area of genre analysis is the identification of the visual imagery, the iconography, of the genre. The romantic comedy is not as immediately recognisable in this respect as are some other genres, such as the western, the gangster film and horror, for example. With these genres we have a clear understanding of the genre-specific settings, props and costume. Certainly the romcom tends to feature urban settings, domestic spaces, often desirable apartments, restaurants and other social spaces. Cavell comments that the romantic comedy also 'requires a setting ... in which the pair have the leisure to be together ... A natural setting is accordingly one of luxury ... work can be postponed without fear of its loss' (1989: 116–17). Brad and Jan venture to a luxurious log cabin in the country for a romantic weekend, with disastrous consequences, in *Pillow Talk*. In *The Holiday*, Iris and Amanda's house swap transplants them both into new settings, one luxurious and the other an idyllic English cottage, although initially somewhat too cramped and boring for its LA housesitter. Nevertheless this change in setting leads to them both healing their wounds and finding new love.

The setting need not always be luxurious; notably, in *Bringing Up Baby* Susan and David's relationship is progressed when they are both in the wild dark wood searching for the lost leopard. As Cherry Potter notes, 'as ... in both *The Taming Of The Shrew* and *It Happened One Night*, moonlit nights in the lonely countryside can release atavistic tendencies in the human psyche ... raising the sexual temperament' (2002: 31–32). Through being removed from civilisation, the couple start to discover their natural instincts and desires, away from the encumbrances and pressures of their everyday lives.

The paraphernalia of romance plays an inevitable role – flowers, chocolates and candlelight – being part of the fantasy appeal of the genre. The telephone can often be an important narrative device, being at the heart of the conflict in *Pillow Talk*, as Brad and Jan are forced to share a phone line. *One Fine Day* uses the device of a mix-up over mobile phones as one of the misunderstandings and disasters that bring the couple together, and in *27 Dresses* Kevin gives Jane a Blackberry which has their song programmed as the ringtone, in order to remind her of him and their wild night singing while standing on the bar.

HISTORY OF THE ROMCOM

Specific phases have been identified in the evolution of the romantic comedy, most notably the screwball comedy and the sex comedy. Nevertheless these particular forms of the genre manifest the same blueprint, and in many respects are not as distinct from each other as the labels seem to imply. These different 'phases' of the genre reflect the social, economic and institutional climate of the time, yet the genre formula is clearly identifiable. Glitre points out how at one time several 'cycles' of the genre may be evident: '*His Girl Friday* may be referred to as a screwball comedy, a career woman comedy, or a comedy of remarriage … ' (2006: 21). With contemporary cinema it seems that the genre has become more fragmented in its nature, with diverse forms seeking to speak to a proliferation of audiences, yet common themes, narratives and tropes can be discerned.

The roots of the romantic comedy genre can be traced back to Shakespeare's comedies. The 'battle of the sexes', the misunderstandings and disguises, farcical situations and the happy ending are all to be found here. Potter comments on how Shakespearian comedies teeter between comedy and disaster, 'balancing on the precarious tightrope between the light and dark side of relationships' (2002: xv). She traces a line back from the romcom to *The Taming of the Shrew* in particular, with its reversal of gender characteristics, the 'sparring partners', the feisty, extraordinary heroine and the need for her energy to be diverted into passionate devotion to her lover.

Screwball comedy

In terms of film history the romcom has been seen as having its origins in the marital comedies of the 1910s and 1920s, particularly the films of Cecil B. De Mille. His 'marital comedies', such as *Old Wives For New* and *Don't Change Your Husband*, address the changing attitudes to sex and romance in the wake of the First World War, with a moving away from Victorian values. The conventions of screwball comedy can be traced back to earlier forms of popular entertainment prevalent in Edwardian and Victorian times: theatre and vaudeville, fiction, and silent film. Yet the first universally acknowledged screwball comedies of the 1930s seemed to bring something fresh and original to cinema audiences, making them a box office success, and setting in place a blueprint for subsequent romcoms.

It Happened One Night and 20th Century were both released in 1934, sharing common elements that heralded a new style of comedy, which came to be known as the screwball comedy. A warring couple are placed in the centre of the narrative and are responsible for the madcap escapades, chaos, slapstick and witty, fast-paced dialogue that marks the progress of their explosive relationship. The term 'screwball' was first applied to describe the heroines of these films, suggesting a crazy energy and a certain nonconformity, but by the late 1930s was used by critics to label the genre. 'Screwball comedy' is a term that has been used very loosely, sometimes being synonymous with romantic comedy. It is also clear that the screwball enjoyed a very finite period of popularity, from 1934 until the Second World War, when its concerns and social milieu suddenly seemed dated. Glitre notes that the narrative is set in an upper-class world, full of glamour and privilege. The couple are mismatched, representing more than just a battle of the sexes, but a collision of lifestyle, values and social class: 'eccentric ... heiresses mingle with journalists, professors and detectives' (2006: 25).

The social context of the screwball comedy is of key importance in understanding its appeal, its representations and its themes. America was in the grip of the Great Depression, the populace were suffering enormous privation and economic misery. The very foundations of society were tested, as men struggled to find work to provide for their families. Screwball comedy offered energy, fun and playfulness, a world where chaos reigned supreme and resulted in happiness and hope for its hero and heroine. This was clearly in strong contrast to the harsh realities of life in mid-1930s America, offering an exhilarating sense of escapism and, ultimately, optimism, as the audience remain comfortable in the knowledge that out of the chaos there will be a happy ending.

The representations of relationships are also reassuring: in the face of the social meltdown of the Depression years, the screwball comedy reaffirms the value of romance and marriage. The 1930s witnessed a reaction to the liberal mores of the previous decade, with a new conservatism in the face of the economic pressures on family life and a return to more traditional gender roles and an emphasis on family values. Nevertheless, the screwball heroine tended to be strong, outspoken and independent, a radical representation for the times, although the narrative would see her brought back into line to some extent, as she settled down to become part of the couple.

Elizabeth Kendall, in her study of 'Depression-era romantic comedies', *The Runaway Bride* (1990) suggests how these films were the Hollywood response to the economic meltdown. The rich had to be represented as flawed and troubled, the less-privileged as being in touch with their instincts and as being essential to the emotional well-being of society: 'This genre used the heroine to articulate the good impulses at the bottom of the American soul ... [it] responded to their audiences' loss of faith by making a virtue of personality traits usually thought of as feminine ... an unashamed belief in the validity of emotions' (3–4). Kendall asserts that these films delivered a message about the possibility of reconciliation, between the sexes, between social classes and between different lifestyles. More importantly, they were films that were unique in terms of being an open exploration of American society. We travel with Ellie (Claudette Colbert) in *It Happened One Night* on her journey through a diminished America, leaving behind her privileged existence and mingling with the proletariat, whether it be singing on the bus or standing in line for the wash facilities.

Her journey results in greater self-knowledge and happiness; our upper-class heroine learns important life lessons by living amongst the poor and needy.

The outbreak of war resulted in a gradual shifting of emphasis as the screwball comedy evolved to reflect the times. Hollywood generally lags behind events and social changes, tending to take time to catch up in representing wider concerns in its output. Screwball comedies continued

Figure 1.2 Ellie chooses to queue with the proletariat in Depression-era America in *It Happened One Night*.

to deal with the glamour and shenanigans of the American upper classes into the 1940s, as in the Preston Sturges films *The Palm Beach Story* and *The Lady Eve*. With the outbreak of the Second World War, with America joining the hostilities in 1941, the themes and narratives shifted, reflecting a concern with the new gender politics stemming from the movement of women out of the home and into work. Films such as *His Girl Friday*, *Woman Of The Year* and *Adam's Rib* explore what happens when a woman penetrates a man's world and the domestic war of the sexes enters the workplace.

The birth of screwball comedy occurred at the same time as the imposition of the strictures of the Production Code, in 1934. This came to be known as the Hays Code, after the president of the Motion Picture Producers and Distributors of America, Will Hays. It was Hollywood's attempt to introduce regulation, in response to public and religious pressures following the more excessive and liberal representation of sex and relationships in the 1920s. Many films of the 'roaring twenties' had upset significant organisations with representations of 'bootleg liquor, jazz music, flappers and wild parties' (Bordwell and Thompson, 1994: 160). There had also been a number of high-profile Hollywood scandals involving the exposure of sordid details of the lifestyle of celebrated actors and filmmakers. The code consisted of a list of rules as to what could and could not be shown in film, censoring representations of sex and adultery, stating that the sanctity of marriage and the home had to be upheld and forbidding unnecessary scenes of passion.

The screwball comedy avoided explicit sexual content, yet sex remained the 'elephant in the corner', as its unspoken presence loomed in the playing out of desires and relationships. There is often a 'know-ingness' in the script and performances which enables an audience to read more into the film than what is made explicit. *Bringing Up Baby* gains much comedy from the double entendre of Professor David Huxley's missing bone as he seeks to complete his dinosaur skeleton.

Figure 1.3 Professor Huxley seeks a missing bone to complete his dinosaur in *Bringing Up Baby*.

Sex is very much part of the screwball comedy, but remains a tension and merely a suggestion that enhances the electricity between the warring couple. By the late 1950s the Production Code's grip on Hollywood had weakened, ushering in the era of the sex comedy.

Sex comedy

Romantic comedy lost its impetus from the 1940s until the mid-1950s. Although still a popular genre, it did not command the same critical and popular status as at the height of the screwball comedy. American society had undergone a sustained period of revisionism in terms of gender relations, in the wake of the War, and at a time of conservative politics and xenophobia. The publication of the Kinsey report into *Sexual Behaviour in the Human Female* in 1953 was symptomatic of a gradual change in attitudes to sex in the 1950s. The same year saw the publication of the first *Playboy* magazine, along with the release of the controversially racy *The Moon Is Blue*, which openly defied the Production Code Administration.

The Moon Is Blue tells the story of a young woman who becomes the object of desire for a young bachelor and his ex-fiancee's father. The chaste yet sexually curious heroine is outspoken and confident in her attitude towards men, creating havoc as the two men strive to seduce her. Otto Preminger refused to bow to pressure to tone down the script, resulting in the refusal of the Production Code Administration to pass the picture because of its racy language and suggestive content. They particularly objected to the use of the words 'seduce', 'virgin' and 'mistress'. Nevertheless, United Artists released the film anyway and it was a great success at the box office, exposing the reduced power of the PCA, which was clearly out of tune with the American audience. To further erode the status of the PCA, the film was nominated for three Oscars, marking the positive reception the film received from within the film industry itself.

The success of *The Moon Is Blue* and the acknowledgement of the possibility of female desire and sexual pleasure led to greater freedoms in the representation of relationships, as seen in sex comedies such as *The Tender Trap* and *Pillow Talk*. These films revolved around the narrative of both the man and the woman wanting sex, and the conflict created by the woman wanting marriage first, whereas the man wants his freedom. Despite being called sex comedies, there was little in the way of overt sex within the narratives, and the films tended to be rather coy in actually tackling this area head on. The narrative situation is very familiar when looked at alongside earlier romcoms, revolving around the 'battle of the sexes'. Little has changed in many respects from the screwball comedies, excepting the cultural and social stakes.

Yet, as Neale and Krutnik point out, there are critical differences between the screwball and the sex comedy, observing that 'romance and courtship become increasingly displaced by an emphasis on sex and seduction' (1990: 169). The narrative revolves more around the bedroom, with the hero striving to seduce the woman, who often remains oblivious as to the machinations that seek to overcome her resistance. Neale and Krutnik go on to point out that the sex comedy has moved away from the sense of play that pervades the screwball comedy, where the couple joust and tease, forming a mutual understanding and profound connectedness. The 1950s romantic comedy tends to represent a 'union more forced than developed' (1990: 170), seemingly founded on sexual attraction and the challenge to the male constituted by the seemingly resistant female. The sex comedy reduces relationships to their basics: sex and procreation. Often the films conclude with marriage and children, as if to reassure the audience that the desirable virgin and the virile bachelor are now the same as them, with all the trappings of a respectable American family unit. This was the era of the baby boom, which witnessd a massive hike in the birth rate, with couples getting married in their early twenties and quickly having their first children. To be unmarried was unnatural. Jerri Jordan (Jayne Mansfield) in *The Girl Can't Help It* expresses the zeitgeist in her yearning to be a mother and wife, deliberately concealing her ability to sing so as to try to resist her lover's attempts to make her into a star.

Much as with screwball comedies, the period of popularity for this genre cycle was finite; the introduction of oral contraception in the early 1960s, along with the social upheaval of the 'swinging sixties', quickly dated the fundamental tenet of the films, that is, the idea of withholding sex and the comedy that ensues. Although there were isolated examples of romantic comedies throughout the rest of the decade, they did not enjoy the same measure of popularity, with either the audience or the film industry.

Nervous comedy

The next significant stage in the evolution of the genre was with the emergence of the 'nervous' comedies of the late 1970s, most notably the films of Woody Allen such as *Annie Hall* and *Manhattan*. These films reflected the angst and world-weariness of the period, where there is no longer any certainty about relationships and identity, and happy endings are rejected in favour of greater realism. Allen's films do not offer easy pleasures for a mass audience, with their references to other art works, criticism and psychoanalysis. The romcom formula is disrupted and ultimately rejected, as the central characters seek to make some sense out of existence and relationships. Marriage is no longer an important goal for the characters, and sex has become a central force in the forging of relationships. Nevertheless there is a powerful sense of nostalgia evoked within these films as characters strive to form meaningful and lasting relationships, which have increasingly come to be regarded as mythical and unrealistic in an ephemeral society.

The resurgence of the romantic comedy

The late 1980s saw a resurgence in the popularity of romantic comedies within mainstream cinema, a popularity which shows little sign of abating. Films such as *Working Girl*, *When Harry Met Sally* and *Sleepless in Seattle* have been labelled 'new romances' or even 'neo-traditional romances' (Jeffers McDonald, 2007), reflecting a concern with traditional models of heterosexual relationships and a desire for more conventional and old-fashioned pairings. These films steadfastly reject the downbeat endings of the nervous romance in favour of fantastical happy endings, when seemingly impossible obstacles have been overcome so that the couple can be together. The continued popularity of the genre seems to suggest an enduring concern regarding gender roles and family structures; the films seem to embrace a mythical bygone age where true love can overcome everything, and offer a solution to our personal crises. This is against a backdrop of soaring divorce rates, ever-growing numbers of single parent families and breakdown in traditional family structures. The emergence of the Aids crisis in the 1980s added to this sense of uncertainty and pessimism regarding sex and relationships. The romcom at the end of the twentieth century embraces the traditional in the face of change and crisis in our emotional relationships.

One way in which some contemporary romantic comedies seek to satisfy their audience is in providing new templates for family structures and relationships. My Best Friend's Wedding finishes with Julia Roberts happy with her gay best friend and Juno sees the teenage mum, having given her child away for adoption, back with her dorky boyfriend. The romantic comedy has renewed and reinvigorated itself by targeting different audiences, most successfully by integrating elements of gross-out comedy and appealing to male audiences, with films such as Knocked Up and There's Something About Mary. In line with the rest of Hollywood output, there has been some effort to recognise the global nature of today's audiences, with actors from ethnic minorities being cast in central roles; notable here are the prolific romantic comedy output of Jennifer Lopez, Will Smith as a 'date doctor' in Hitch, and Queen Latifah as an escaped convict in Bringing Down The House, a problematic film in that it avoids the sensitive issue of an interracial coupling of the central protagonists by having Latifah's character paired up with the Jewish best friend of the male protagonist.

Despite repeated warnings that the genre is exhausted, it continues to maintain momentum. In 1978 Brian Henderson pronounced that

Table 1.1 Top ten grossing romantic comedies (since 1978)

Rank	Title/year	Lifetime gross ($ million)	Screens
1	My Big Fat Greek Wedding (2002)	241	2016
2	What Women Want (2000)	183	3092
3	Hitch (2005)	179	3575
4	Pretty Woman (1990)	178	1811
5	There's Something About Mary (1998)	176	2555
6	The Proposal (2009)	163	3158
7	Sex And The City (2008)	153	3325
8	Runaway Bride (1999)	152	3240
9	Knocked Up (2007)	149	2975
10	As Good As It Gets (1997)	148	1837

Source: boxofficemojo.com

the genre was on the verge of extinction, yet it has proved him rather premature, having gone from strength to strength as the twentieth century came to its end, and is still proving to be a box office favourite, as can be seen from Table 1.1.

It seems foolish to claim that the genre will ever die, as it revolves around perennial themes – romance, relationships, identity – that have always been part of our shared culture, whether literature, theatre or film. The genre explores themes and issues that are central to the experience and desires of the audience, yet it simultaneously evolves to reflect shifts in the audience, industry and society.

2

THE HEROINE OF THE ROMANTIC COMEDY

Romantic comedy has always been thought of as a women's genre, although there continue to be exceptions to this, most markedly in the recent films of Judd Apatow, but also in the work of Woody Allen. Nevertheless the heroine is central to the appeal of the genre to its audience and, as with many film heroines, a female spectator may seek someone to identify with, but also someone who embodies dreams and desires. Yet the romantic comedy heroine is almost always the construct resulting from the work of men, due to the patriarchal nature of the film industry, creating a tension in the representations. Increasingly there have been female directors of romantic comedies, for example Nora Ephron (*Sleepless In Seattle*, *You've Got Mail*) and Anne Fletcher (*27 Dresses*, *The Proposal*), yet they remain in a minority. The earliest romantic comedies were notable in involving a number of female writers, such as Vina Delmar (*The Awful Truth*), Hagar Wilde (*Bringing Up Baby* and *I Was A Male War Bride*) and Ruth Gordon (*Pat and Mike* and *Adam's Rib*). Certainly, many of the heroines of the screwball era were feisty, fast-talking, no-nonsense characters, yet the majority of the production team were male.

Katharine Hepburn was unusual in the scale of her involvement in many of her films, having significant input into the production process to the extent of even choosing her director and co-star on occasion.

Hepburn was reputed to have rejected a first version of the ending of *Woman Of The Year* in favour of the final version, in which Tess Harding's incompetence as a homemaker serves to cut her down to size. Her husband watches impassively as she struggles to carry out the most basic domestic tasks, witnessing the humiliation of this fabulously talented and capable career woman. The audience are positioned to feel greater sympathy for her husband, played by Spencer Tracy, who has been neglected and taken for granted by his globetrotting wife. The paradox here is that of the powerful female star – who has built a reputation as a feminist icon through her mother's campaigning and her early film roles – using her clout to control her film persona, but ending up by undermining feminist values in creating a representation that will gratify the audience. Hepburn was particularly sensitive about her screen persona, after a series of box office failures, which critics had suggested were a result of a certain gender ambiguity associated with her characters and her 'unsatisfactoriness as a feminine object' (Glitre, 2006: 114).

THE SCREWBALL HEROINE

The heroine of the screwball comedy can be seen as oddly radical, given the general tone of the 1930s. She is spirited and determined, she is prepared to manipulate and deceive in order to get her man, she is fiercely independent and knows her own mind, yet she can only attain happiness through having the love of a man. Apparently in defiance of these many attributes of a strong woman, the genre can be argued to be innately conservative in this respect. The screwball heroine is crazy and unpredictable, she is capable of throwing a man's life into complete chaos, and has excessive energies and exuberance. In this respect she is a threat to society and needs to be contained by the restraints of marriage. This excessiveness is exhilarating for the audience, there's a sense of real freedom and rebellion against the stuffiness of social constraints. Given the backdrop of the Depression, the radical nature of the female central character may have been particularly appealing for the audience, as they were shackled by social and economic realities making day-to-day life less than exhilarating. The most devastating stock market collapse in American history had taken place in 1929, resulting in a worldwide economic slump which lasted for a decade, with mass unemployment and serious financial difficulties for many families.

The influence of Mae West's emergence as a major star in 1933 can be seen in the screwball heroine. Her two films from that year, *She Done Him Wrong* and *I'm No Angel*, were huge box office hits, their appeal centring on her extraordinary persona, the original disruptive woman who dominates the screen space with her overt sexuality, her sassy dialogue and command of her fate. This exuberance and forcefulness is made explicit in the screwball heroine. She strides across the screen, wearing the most fantastic and eye-catching outfits; she challenges the other characters with fast-paced and witty repartee, never seeming to back down. Irene Bullock (Carole Lombard) wears extraordinary trouser suits and gowns made of the most vivid fabric designs in *My Man Godfrey*, whilst Susan's (Katharine Hepburn) confident and athletic stride commands attention and challenges the status quo in *Bringing Up Baby*. Hildy (Rosalind Russell) fires insults and repartee across the screen in *His Girl Friday*, whilst Jean (Barbara Stanwyck) drops an apple on Charles's (Henry Fonda) head in *The Lady Eve*. All of these characters command attention and demand results, being seemingly irrepressible.

At the same time, the heroine uses her body to ensnare and captivate, whether it be Jean bewitching Charles with her shapely legs as he is grovelling at her feet, or Claudette Colbert flashing her legs in order to procure a lift. Irene in *My Man Godfrey* contrives to seduce Godfrey (William Powell) by swooning, prompting him to take the drastic measure of hoisting her over his shoulders in a commanding way, carrying her up to her boudoir, where he lays her on her bed. Irene is clearly very sexy in her clinging dress, and this is heightened as he places her under a cold shower. Irene's efforts to seduce Godfrey are foiled, yet the scene purveys a powerful sexual tone and clearly enforces atavistic instincts as the man roughly manhandles the woman, carrying her to

Figure 2.1 Jean bewitches Charles in *The Lady Eve*.

the bedroom. The comedy is created by Godfrey's realisation that he is being tricked, and his ensuing action in placing her under the cold shower. She is punished, the cold water quelling her desires. In this scene Godfrey clearly takes a paternal role, in admonishing and punishing the wayward Irene, and in turn, Irene enjoys and respects his moral rectitude. The Bullock household lacks an effective parental presence, both of the daughters having been spoilt and indulged, as Godfrey points out to Irene's petulant sister. Even Alexander Bullock, the father of this 'crazy' family, welcomes the calm guiding influence of Godfrey as he supplants the father by saving the family from poverty and teaching both daughters a valuable lesson.

Irene Bullock is typical of the heiress heroine of the screwball comedy in ostensibly having everything, but realising that this is nothing in comparison with the love of a good man, a man who can guide her in a way that her own family have failed to. She is prepared to sacrifice her family and fortune for the love of a man, much as the heroine of It Happened One Night, Ellie (Claudette Colbert), who runs away from the privilege and wealth of her father's world to finally find a new protector, who teaches her invaluable life lessons, enabling her to grow to a new, mature wisdom.

The screwball heroine tends to come from a fractured or dysfunctional family, often being motherless and having a weak father figure who fails to contain his daughter. The hero is a knight in shining armour who can offer moral certainty and structure where her family have failed. To a 1930s audience this offers a particularly appealing scenario, as government and society have failed them, perpetuating the Hollywood myth of the possibility of redemption and resolution. Many of the films centre on a woman who wants to be taken in hand, who wants a man who can control and contain her. Characters such as Ellie and Susan Vance are very ready to relinquish their indulged positions within a wealthy family for a man who is a social inferior but is morally superior. The heroine is represented as incomplete, leading an empty life. Irene and her social set in *My Man Godfrey* fill their lives with meaningless frivolities, such as the scavenger hunt, which results in their combing the city dump for the trophy of the 'forgotten man'. LaCava represents the empty-headed rich in a harsh, unforgiving light as they bray and shriek, desperate to win the pointless competition, brandishing their 'useless objects', albeit a goat, or a tramp. Ellie in *It Happened One Night* is trapped on her father's luxurious yacht, driven to marrying the unsuitable King Westley purely to defy her father and to assert a measure of independence.

The screwball comedy heroine tends to encapsulate a certain independence of spirit, though, in rejecting the father and the expectations of her social class and opting instead for the 'common man', with whom the audience can identify. That said, the 'common man' is only common in terms of not always coming from the privilege and wealth of the upper classes, and is very 'uncommon' in terms of character and personal traits. The heroine is stubborn and headstrong, showing a strength of will and character in asserting her wishes and desires. In some ways it could be said that the narrative of these films, in impelling the heroine towards the resolution of marriage, serves to reinforce the status quo. The destabilising force of the independent woman is brought back into the fold, under the guidance of a new father figure in the form of her husband-to-be. The women have an adventurous spirit which manifests itself in the madcap antics they are involved in. Reflecting the label of 'screwball' for this stage of the genre, these antics challenge society's boundaries on what is normal behaviour. Ellie hurls herself off the side of the yacht, launching herself into the real world where she no longer has the protection of her wealth, and has to survive on her wits. Lucy (Irene Dunne), in The Awful Truth, has been out all night with her singing teacher, Armand Duval, much to the disgust of her husband. Susan Vance, in Bringing Up Baby, is the apotheosis of this crazy, independent woman who hunts down her quarry, in the form of the hapless Professor David Huxley.

Glitre (2006: 27) comments as to how the screwball loses its innocence in the early 1940s as the character of the headstrong heiress is replaced by the more calculating woman, who schemes to entrap the man. Jean is typical of this type as the female confidence trickster in The Lady Eve, who uses her feminine wiles to seduce and manipulate the fabulously wealthy and naive Hopsie. Despite her criminal past and cynical ploys, she wins her man. Whereas the 1930s screwball comedy is considered by some as a celebration of femininity, the 1940s sees increasing questioning of this, with the man as a victim, or even needing to teach the woman a lesson. The lesson has changed, as the woman has to be cut down to size as she overreaches herself with her zestful independence, as in the Katharine Hepburn comedies, The Philadelphia Story and Woman of the Year. James Harvey believes that there is a reversal of 'the old screwball pattern ... It was no longer the witty heroine who had the edge but the feet-on-the-ground hero' (1987: 409). Natural order is restored as the heroine submits to the hero's sense and strength of will.

In many ways, these films can be seen to attempt to defuse the gender tensions created by the Second World War, as men are lauded as heroes whilst the women strive to undertake men's work at home. Ultimately the War led to a redefinition of gender roles, as women were encouraged to leave the home and make a contribution to the war effort. Millions of women were needed in America to fill the gap left by the men needed to fight the War; these women were required to undertake employment which was normally carried out by men, in jobs from which women were formerly excluded. Many of these women were married, even though it was effectively taboo for married women to remain in the workplace, the expectation being that their job was to look after the home and family. It was made clear that this was purely a patriotic effort in order to support the war effort, and that normal gender roles would be resumed when the troops came home. Films such as *Woman of the Year* and *Adam's Rib* feature independent career women who are represented as deviant and unnatural, yet who are redeemed by the power of love, returning them to their natural state in respecting male power and primacy.

THE SEX COMEDY HEROINE

The 1950s witnessed a post-war baby boom, with the woman's place being firmly back in the home. The American Dream was resurrected during this period of prosperity, as the reinvigorated ideal of family life was bolstered by greater material wealth. The domestic idyll was all that the American woman was assumed to be interested in, sacrificing education and career prospects for the fulfilment of being a wife and mother. The sex comedy reflected a new uncertainty in terms of gender roles, in the wake of the growing awareness of sex itself as a response to the impact of the Kinsey Report on *Sexual Behaviour in the Human Female*. The Report was very much at odds with society's attitudes, as it revealed that women were sexually active and, what is more, were often having carnal knowledge of men before marriage!

The heroine of the sex comedy emerged out of this tension between the reality and the fantasy of femininity that was prevalent in America. On the one hand she is capable of desire, yet on the other she yearns for the domestic idyll of marriage and all that it entails, in terms of husband, children, house and consumer goods. The typical heroine has desires, but within the parameters of maintaining the domestic status quo, in contrast to the hero, whose reluctance to commit can be almost pathological. She may well work, often in some suitably feminine capacity – for example Jan is an interior decorator in *Pillow Talk* – but her goal is marriage. As Julie (Debbie Reynolds) declares in *The Tender Trap*: 'I mean a career is just fine, but it's no substitute for marriage … A woman isn't really a woman at all until she's been married and had children. And why? Because she's fulfilled.'

The 1950s romantic comedies displayed this disparate attitude towards women, the central characters been divided between the two opposing archetypes, the virgin and the whore. Doris Day epitomised the former type, being branded in her later roles as the 'world's oldest virgin'. She was safe and reassuring for the female audience, with her veneer of ordinariness. In her film roles her character espoused values that the housewife could relate to: the desire for marriage and domestic bliss, with the possibility of true love. Marilyn Monroe's roles in *The Seven Year Itch* and *Some Like It Hot* encapsulated the antithesis of the virgin, purveying sexuality and a sense of availability, combined with a childlike demeanour, which alleviated the threat of such an excess of femininity. Glitre comments as to how this hyper-sexualised image of womanhood becomes ridiculous in its excessiveness, citing Jayne Mansfield in her role as Jerri Jordan in *The Girl Can't Help It*, with her impressive curves which mesmerise and disempower all the men in her path. Yet Jerri declares: 'I just want to be a wife, have kids – but everyone figures me for a sexpot. No one thinks I'm equipped for motherhood!'

Ultimately both archetypes have the same aim, an aim which reinforces the status quo, placing the woman very much in the home. The heroine of the sex comedy lacks the strength of spirit and will that was manifest in her sisters in the screwball era. She can be feisty and has her own agenda in opposition to the man, but she tends to be passive and compliant. Jerri Jordan takes this type to an extreme, being very much the prototype for the 'dumb blonde'. She walks with an oddly pronounced wiggle, and is prone to gurgling at the end of her sentences. Her face is largely vacant, reflecting a complete absence of detectable intelligence: Jerri is just about as close to an inflatable doll as a woman can be. She is only happy when cooking for others, and wants nothing more than to procreate. She is made miserable by the prospect of developing a career as a singer, and finishes the film content as a wife who cannot take her eyes off her husband, and as a mother of numerous children. Jerri is fundamentally a caricature of a woman, created primarily for the male gaze, in line with the target audience for this rock and roll romantic comedy.

EQUAL OPPORTUNITIES ...

The 1960s had seen a sexual revolution, as a new generation rebelled against the conservatism of their parents. Women were supposedly liberated by the availability of oral contraception, campaigning for equal rights in this decade of civil unrest and rebellion. The impact of the 1960s on gender politics is written large in the characterisation of the heroines of the nervous comedies of the 1970s. This period in the evolution of the romantic comedy is significant for its radical questioning of relationships and gender roles, notably in the films of Woody Allen, but also in films such as *Starting Over* and *An Unmarried Woman*. It is noticeable just how few romantic comedies were made at this time; the genre seemed to have been pensioned off as a result of the tumult of the previous decade, Hollywood seeming nonplussed as to how to tackle the themes of love and relationships in the wake of feminism. No longer is the heroine dependent on a man, she is independent and growing in self-confidence, often remaining an enigma to the man. This confidence is manifest in the character of Annie Hall (Diane Keaton) in the eponymous film. She is ambitious and self-centred, indifferent to sex, and ultimately rejects Alvy (Woody Allen). Annie is a dynamic woman who knows what she wants – her character radically challenges the needy heroines of the previous decades. She dresses like a man, in stylish trousers, shirts, ties and waistcoats, and seems to physically dwarf Alvy.

Characters such as Annie have proved to be anomalous in the history of the romcom as the genre matured and re-emerged in the late 1980s, being re-energised by the growing equality of the sexes at the end of the twentieth century. The United Kingdom had its first female prime minister with the election of Margaret Thatcher in 1979 and women seemed to be making gradual progress in being taken seriously in the workplace. The 'new romance', as it was labelled by Frank Krutnik (1998), signalled a return to the traditional narrative and gender roles of the romantic comedy. These films reflect their historical context in representing a fast-moving urban world where women can be successful and competitive in the workplace, yet often at the cost of their emotional and personal lives. They yearn to 'have it all' and have to make significant sacrifices to attain emotional equilibrium. *When Harry Met Sally* follows the relationship between the couple over the span of a decade, during which Sally (Meg Ryan) becomes a successful journalist, has a good lifestyle, apartment and friends, yet can only attain true happiness through marriage to 'the one'. The film reveals an anxiety about not being married and missing out on traditional domestic stability that was very much the propelling concern behind earlier romcoms. As Sally's friend warns her: 'the right man for you may be out there right now, and if you don't grab him someone else will. And you'll have to spend the rest of your life knowing that someone else is married to your husband'.

Working Girl deals more explicitly with contemporary gender issues within the framework of the romcom, seeing Tess (Melanie Griffiths) fight against sexism and class prejudice to gain career success. The narrative hinges on the contrast between the softer, more childlike Tess and the hard-edged, successful Katharine (Sigourney Weaver), who is ruthless and manipulative. Tess is represented as being very much in touch with her femininity, in contrast to Katharine, who is a threat to both men and women in her single-minded pursuit of her objectives. Katharine loses her job and her man, whereas Tess is rewarded for her hard work by gaining a doting partner and the job she craved. At the close of the film we see Jack (Harrison Ford) packing a lunchbox for

Tess, in an interesting role reversal where the successful, sophisticated partner is supporting and nurturing the career woman. The final scene does not even feature Jack, as Tess is shown enjoying her new office in a soaring skyscraper, establishing her success in achieving her ambitions and the start of a new, exciting phase in her career. For a romantic comedy it is a radical ending, as the man is not present, suggesting a new world in terms of gender and power.

HAVING IT ALL

The heroine of the contemporary romcom does not seem to have moved on much from her generic antecedents. There's a sense of panic in many of the representations of women who are struggling to 'have it all', staring into a relationship abyss as they try to reconcile career with relationships. These heroines are successful in their work and have a loyal group of friends, yet they have failed to find the ideal partner. The majority of these movies will end with the woman making significant sacrifices for a traditional heterosexual partnership; she embraces the romantic dream and is whisked off her feet by the right guy, having realised that love conquers all. Today's romcom heroines are tantalising figures. They live on the cusp between strong, empowered choices and more traditional, reactionary fates. They start the film as powerful, successful and free from the confines of the traditional family. They work and play hard, seemingly living the post-feminist dream. Yet at a decisive point in the narrative, their values are overturned and they can no longer find happiness in their former lifestyle. They realise that their future must be with their significant other, often seeking the confirmation of their new status within all the traditional trappings of commitment: hence the central importance of weddings within the contemporary romcom.

The modern-day heroine learns that she cannot 'have it all', and can only achieve happiness by sacrificing her urge to compete in the male world and coming to terms with her feminine instincts to be married/

coupled and settled. Andi (Kate Hudson) in *How To Lose A Guy In 10 Days* forsakes her dream career move so that she can stay in New York with Ben, after he races after her departing taxi to put a halt to her plans. Tess in *27 Dresses* is the perfect heroine for the twenty-first century: she has been stuck in her dead-end job for years, suffering for her unrequited love for her boss. Kevin rescues her from her Cinderella existence and a life devoted to looking after the needs of others, never putting herself first. When she realises her love for Kevin she immediately quits her job, the only goal being to be with him. Her existence as an independent working woman is represented as superfluous to her real destiny, to be a bride for the right man. Just as in the fairy tales, the modern romantic comedy concludes with a wedding, reinforcing the importance of tradition and conformity.

CASE STUDY: *BRINGING UP BABY*

Bringing Up Baby has become one of the most celebrated of the screwball comedies, yet was an infamous box office disaster at the time. It was critically derided and created a loss in excess of $300 000 for RKO Pictures. Nevertheless, it seemed a promising formula on paper, combining the proven screwball talents of Cary Grant, fresh from the success of *The Awful Truth*, and director Howard Hawks, responsible for one of the very first screwballs with *20th Century*. Yet the film was panned for being formulaic and far-fetched, taking screwball comedy too far! Another major problem with the film was Katharine Hepburn, who was in a difficult period of her career, having had a series of flops. Her performance resulted in her being called 'box office poison' and led to the conclusion of her time at RKO, whilst Hawks also had his contract terminated.

The film starts with Professor David Huxley who is about to marry Alice Swallow, but meets Susan Vance on the golf course, where she proceeds to wreck his business meeting and his chances of securing important funding for his museum. They bump into each other again and proceed to get entangled in each other's lives, especially when Susan loses her pet leopard. Susan realises that she loves David and contrives to get him to miss his wedding. Ultimately David is dumped by his fiancée, and he and Susan declare their feelings to each other at the very end of the film.

The plot is centred on the 'warring couple', who are seemingly incongruous yet instantly are caught up in each other's lives, as if a net has descended over the two of them, and as they struggle to disentangle themselves they become more caught up in their inevitable shared fate. The film is filled with references to hunting and prey; Susan sets various lures and traps in order to 'capture' David, the two of them spend a lot of the film pursuing animals, and David is introduced to Susan's aunt as a big game hunter. Ultimately the majority of the characters end up trapped in prison, as a result of a chain of misunderstandings.

The nature of the relationship between David and Susan is prefigured in the meet-cute, where Susan hijacks David's golf ball and his car, ruining his chance of gaining a million dollars for his museum by impressing his golfing partner. The encounter is typical of the confusion and slapstick that dominates the narrative, it demonstrates the excessive nature of the screwball comedy, as their relationship leaves a wake of breakages and damage, whether it be the rock that mistakenly hits the lawyer's head or the damage to David's car after Susan forcibly uses it as a battering ram to get out of the parking spot.

The relationship begins with a sequence of arguments and misunderstandings, but then moves into a second phase when Susan realises that David is the man for her, and then sets out to make him realise this. The film ends with David's recognition of his love for Susan and the two embrace amongst the wreckage of his former life, as his beloved brontosaurus skeleton is destroyed, inadvertently, by Susan's actions. David's priorities have changed, his work is no longer his life, he has discovered love and, simultaneously, fun. For the film puts emphasis on the importance of fun and play being significant in a happy relationship. David's declaration of love for Susan reflects this:

I ought to thank you […] You see, I've just discovered that was the best day that I've ever had in my whole life […] I've never had a better time […] I love you, I think.

This realisation that there is more to life than old bones signifies a regression from the responsibilities of adulthood to the carefree playfulness of a new state of immaturity, embracing the fun and freedom that Susan introduces into his life. This is in stark contrast to the repressed nature of his fiancée, Miss Swallow, who scolds David when he suggests a honeymoon, in the opening scene:

MISS SWALLOW: Now once and for all David nothing must interfere with your work. Our marriage must entail no domestic entanglements of any kind.
DAVID: Oh … you mean, you mean …
MISS SWALLOW: I mean of any kind David.
DAVID: Oh Alice, I was sorta hoping that … You mean children and all that sort of thing?
MISS SWALLOW: Exactly. This … [gestures towards brontosaurus] … will be our child. Yes David, I see our marriage as purely a dedication to your work.

These two scenes bookend the film, reinforcing the contrast between the two women: Miss Swallow and Susan Vance. The former is strict and disciplined in her appearance, movement and voice, whereas Susan is effusive and undisciplined, suggesting freedom and energy. Miss Swallow has her hair pulled back into a severe style, her clothes are dark and restrained, her jacket is buttoned up, and she wears glasses, creating a fiercely professional demeanour. She hectors David, speaking to him as to a child, forcing him to toe the line, remaining unsmiling and severe. Miss Swallow is the humourless essence of the career woman who figures so largely in many 1940s romcoms. She is represented as being unnatural, there is no sense of romance and intimacy allowed by her in their relationship; she doesn't want children, she is dedicated to her work, and her marriage is to be an extension of this. She is a repressive force in the narrative, reflecting the social unease of the 1930s around gender roles, with the backlash against the progress of women's rights in the 1920s.

Susan Vance is the antithesis of all that Miss Swallow represents. On the one hand, Susan encapsulates glamour and the feminine, but at the same time she is a radical, free spirit who can be seen to challenge society in various ways. This contradictory nature reflects the star persona of Katharine Hepburn. Many of her former roles built on her public image of the trouser-wearing descendant of a liberal and privileged East Coast family, her mother having being prominent in the suffragette movement. Hepburn was decidedly unconventional and headstrong, coming from a very different background to most Hollywood leading women. This is the animus that drives the Susan who strides confidently across the golf course, who doesn't balk at the idea of a pet leopard, and who is prepared to go to any length to get her

Figure 2.2 Susan is the glamorous free spirit in Bringing Up Baby.

man, taking the initiative throughout the film. Susan is prepared to lie, steal and even masquerade as a gangster in order to get what she wants. She is a radical and chaotic force, even before she has fallen for David, as we see when she commandeers his golf ball and his car, effectively carrying him off, as she drives away with him stuck on the running board. In an interesting instance of role reversal, she literally sweeps him off his feet and carries him away; he is helpless in the face of her energy and will.

Susan is a conventional heroine of the screwball comedy in her role as the rich girl who falls for a man from an inferior social class, although the theme of social inequality is not as central to the film as in earlier screwball comedies such as *My Man Godfrey* and *It Happened One Night*. Nevertheless, Susan is represented as being privileged and having no guiding disciplinary force in her life – only the admonishments of her aunt, Mrs Random. Susan is a fantasy figure for the audience, as she leads a life of easy luxury, having no demands on her time, resplendent in a range of glamorous outfits. It is as if she is above the law as she steals a car, or masquerades as 'Swingin' Door Susie' in order to elude the cops. She has a confidence that overcomes all that gets in her way, but with a childlike innocence in delighting in the situations she finds herself in, and relishing the moment with a naivety and essential goodness that alleviates any blame for her wrongdoings. She just wants what she knows should be hers, her playmate, David, although he is oblivious of his destiny. In this respect she demonstrates the feminine wiles that we see in other screwball heroines, such as Irene in *My Man Godfrey* and Jean in *The Lady Eve*. Susan pretends she is being attacked by the leopard whilst on the phone to David in order to bring him running to her rescue, and she sends his clothes away to the cleaners whilst he's in the shower in order to keep him with her. Her duplicity is excused, though, as we see that she is possessed by her love for David, as she admits to him in the final scene: 'All that happened happened because I was trying to keep you near me, and I just did anything that came into my head. I'm so sorry.' Again, Susan leads the way in declaring her feelings, she is transparent and in touch with her own emotions, conforming to the feminine archetype, whereas David has to undergo a sequence of ordeals and be dumped by his fiancée in order to recognise the truth.

Susan's characterisation encompasses the glamour and femininity that defines the heroine of the screwball comedy. The woman is seemingly irrational and a chaotic force, yet is decorative and sensitive, ultimately motivated solely by her love for the man. Susan is resplendent in extraordinary gowns and evening dresses, soft fabrics float around her, silky materials cling to her to accentuate her physicality. Her appeal is heightened in the farcical scene when David mistakenly rips the back of her gown, exposing her and making her vulnerable in a public place. Generally it is Susan who is in control and who creates the chaos and humiliation, having to step in and save David, yet here she is the damsel in distress, as she is later on when David has to save her from the leopard, declaring 'Oh you're wonderful … you're absolutely wonderful! You're a hero, you've saved my life! Oh, you will go down in history, I've never seen such bravery!' David's heroism is undermined as he faints immediately after this, falling into the arms of Susan, and her words seem quite ironic, given the stuffy reality of Professor David Huxley.

The representation of gender is not straightforward, it can be seen as somewhat progressive, given the social context of the film, yet in many ways it serves to support the contemporary ideologies concerning the roles of men and women. David saves Susan at the end of the film: as his brontosaurus falls to the ground, he hoists her onto the platform, in a final manly gesture. Yet she has led to the collapse of his edifice and has captured her prey. Susan is represented as childlike, needing an authority figure to give her parameters for her carefree, chaotic existence. She pursues David everywhere, being anxious to please, refusing to be put off by David's disapproval and annoyance. She echoes his words until he tells her off, giggling and imploring in a childish tone.

Molly Haskell describes Susan Vance as a typical 'Hawksian woman', suggesting that the female leads in Howard Hawks's 1930s comedies are strong heroic types 'who are more at ease with their bodies when the bodies are in motion, doing things. They do not cultivate seductive poses ... ' (1987: 138). Susan is a doer, she makes the romance happen and takes charge of David's fate, although ultimately she is hidebound by her generic destiny to recognise only a future with a significant other. Haskell points out that 'Intelligence was a salient feature of the Hawksian heroine' (1987: 139) and that this defines the nature of the fast-paced, witty dialogue which is a trademark feature of the screwball comedy. The advent of sound enabled the woman to speak and to have a character and thoughts that animated performance beyond merely being a spectacle.

CASE STUDY: *SEX AND THE CITY*

Sex And The City, the movie, was a box office triumph in 2008. It commanded the highest-ever opening weekend box office in the United States for a movie headed by women, and is described as the 'first ever tent pole blockbuster to rest squarely on a female demographic' (Setoodeh, 2008). Nevertheless it met with the general critical disdain which is very much part of the territory for the romantic comedy. Male critics revelled in the opportunity to castigate the terrain of this franchise, as it garnered approval ratings one would associate with the most egregious tripe to go straight to video.

The movie is an extension of the television series, which lasted over six seasons, from 1998 until 2004, broadcast on HBO, and was subsequently syndicated around the world. The narrative revolves around the four central women, Carrie (Sarah Jessica Parker), Charlotte (Kristin Davis), Miranda (Cynthia Nixon) and Samantha (Kim Cattrall), and their trials and tribulations regarding relationships. The series was heralded by many as a celebration of strong, feisty, successful women who had clear sense of identity and direction. It was seen to represent the dilemmas facing women at the turn of the century, dealing with the issues regarding sex, love, careers and relationships. Yet a body of opinion condemns the representations of femininity for being unrealistic and even harmful, as the women live in a fantasy bubble, perpetuating an image of femininity as consumers obsessed by shopping and fashion, rarely doing a serious day's work (excepting Miranda – who is routinely punished in the narratives for being rather too 'manly' in her attitudes). They obsess about men, marriage and sex, much like the members of a harem who each eagerly await to be the next 'chosen one', having little more to do in the meantime than bedeck themselves in finery.

The television series conformed to the romantic comedy genre in many ways, centring on the character of Carrie and her protracted struggle to get Mr Big (Chris Noth) to commit to her. The narrative revolves around the search for love, involving the usual complications and mis-understandings. The mise-en-scène is archetypal of the genre, being located in Manhattan, featuring glamorous apartments, extraordinary high fashion and accompanying accessories, nightclubs and cafés. Carrie does not have just one best friend to confide in, but three, and, moreover, a gay male friend … a vital component of the *fin de siècle* romcom. Whereas the romantic comedy often features the 'wrong' partner, *Sex And The City*'s heroines are engaged in a picaresque adventure, encountering a string of possible partners, many of whom are rejected, or reject, in the

Figure 2.3 Rite of passage: Carrie prepares to marry Mr Big in *Sex And The City*.

search for the right partner. The film foregrounds the narrative structure of the romcom, building on the contemporary popularity of the subgenre of the wedding movie. This subgenre has taken the romance's defining rite of passage – the wedding – and placed it at the centre of the narrative, where it becomes the testing ground for a relationship, as in *The Wedding Date* (2002), *Wedding Crashers* (2005) and *27 Dresses* (2008), to name but a few.

The film is structured around rotating storylines which centre on the theme of women negotiating the framework of their relationships with men. The main storyline centres on Carrie and Mr Big's decision to get married, only for him to get cold feet at the last moment. Mr Big abandons Carrie at the altar, resulting in suffering and anger, but also in an opportunity for sober reflection and greater self-knowledge. They split up, but are reunited to get married at the end of the film, remedying all the previous wrongs and suffering. Meanwhile Steve and Miranda also split up, as Steve has been unfaithful to Miranda. They too are reunited at the end, when Miranda realises that she has not been as attentive as she needed to be. Samantha is happily settled with Smith in LA, but then realises that she is not suited to monogamy and leaves him to return to her former life in New York.

The movie certainly perpetuates the powerful post-feminist image of the sisterhood, one of the most iconic images being the four women, arm in arm, sashaying down the street in their eye-catching outfits, clearly at ease and happy, a force to be reckoned with. The women form a mutually supporting 'family', sharing their most intimate thoughts and experiences in the repeated café scenes which punctuate the narrative. The role of the best friend is magnified within the film, so that the centre of gravity for the narrative is moved away from the couple to the best friend. Indeed the rather dull figure of Mr Big is unconvincing and almost redundant in comparison to the compelling female characters. This creates an odd tension within the text as Carrie's happiness and hopes are pinned on the insubstantial absent male, yet she herself is vibrant, intelligent and feisty, and has much healthier, franker relationships with her friends than with her partner. After the romance of the marriage, when Carrie has finally 'captured' her Mr Big, the final scene is notable for his absence. Big is seemingly just part of the scenery for her real life, a necessary emotional backdrop to give her the confidence and happiness to continue with the real business of her existence, her friendships and social life. Indeed, in her profession as a writer on matters of the heart she gains a lot of her material from the suffering, reversals and uncertainties of her relationship with Big; their harmonious coupling could be problematic in actually removing a vital source of inspiration.

Carrie uses the personal lives of her friends as another source of material – as she declares in the opening sequence: 'Year after year, my single girlfriends were my salvation, and ... , as it turned out, my meal ticket,' she is something of a voyeur. In this respect the text has a postmodern self-referentiality, being based on the Candace Bushnell column in the *New York Observer*, which in turn was based on Bushnell's experiences. In the final scene we see the women, without their partners, clearly relishing each other's company, drinking and laughing as they celebrate Samantha's fiftieth birthday. As is typical of the series, Carrie concludes with her thoughts in the voiceover, on the theme of the narrative, in this case, love:

> Maybe some labels are best left in the closet. Maybe when we label people – bride, groom, husband, wife, married, single – we forget to look past the label to the person ... four New York women enter the next phase of their lives, dressed head to toe in love, and that's the one label that never goes in and out of style.

We see each character in turn, in close up, highlighting their pleasure in their shared company, followed by a high-angle tracking shot which encircles the four of them, together, oblivious to anyone else. This is accompanied by the power pop of Jennifer Hudson belting out the anthemic *All Dressed In Love*, reinforcing the theme. The love that Carrie speaks of is primarily for each other, as it is them that we see emphasising the key message of *Sex And The City*, the power and support that can exist in close female friendship which becomes a buffer against the rest of the world. Here, the rest of the world includes their partners, who are peripheralised by the camera and the narrative. Ostensibly, men create the problems; the women support each other in surviving the adversities of love.

The language of this sequence is very telling, revealing what has been argued to be the capitalist ideology of the series. Carrie's closing words pursue a fashion metaphor, as does the Hudson song, promoting the idea that fashion is an expression of self-love and part of how a woman defines herself. The series has been criticised for its explicit espousal of consumerist values, with shopping and designer labels being of central importance in defining the women. Indeed Carrie wryly informs us at the start of the film: 'Having gotten the knack for labels early, I concentrated on the search for love,' prioritising clothes over relationships in terms of her own values. The philosophy of the series is post-feminist, declaring that women can be girly and feminine, but at the same time can have careers and be the equals of men.

Carrie realises that she is culpable for the breakdown in her relationship with Big, because she chose the Vivienne Westwood wedding dress and decided that the wedding needed to be a large event, rather than the intimate occasion that Big desires. She allows herself to be carried away planning the fantasy marriage to suit the dress, and overlooks Big's needs. She is punished for this and has to learn to put him first, to listen to him, rather than just gratifying herself. When she does marry him her outfit is modest and restrained, as *she* has to become, in order to be right for him. Yet we know this is a lie as soon as the doors swing open and she hurls herself, screaming, at her friends, restraint falling by the wayside. In this respect, we see again that Carrie, like the other women, shows exuberance and vitality when with her friends. Relationships are serious, but friendships are fun.

Just as it is fashion that comes between them, it is shoes that bring the couple together. Shoes are very much fetish objects within *Sex And The City*, holding a value and mystical power, in the eyes of Carrie in particular, that encapsulate the commodity fetishism of the series as a whole. It is only the possible loss of a pair of Manolo Blahniks that brings Carrie back to the new apartment, where Big is standing alone, fondling the shoes. The shoes define Carrie as a character, they are expensive, impractical and a triumph of style over substance, perhaps. All of the girls teeter on heels; Charlotte wobbles particularly precariously, and can walk only with great difficulty in some scenes.

Carrie is a child to the adult Big. He indulges her by buying the fantasy apartment, then fitting it out with her dream closet. When she upsets him he retains an air of remote disapproval and is the reproving parent figure who remains detached as she 'plays' with her friends. Big is the serious, weighty adult, always dressed in black, seemingly a good ten years older than her. Carrie has to change and adapt herself to fit in with his ways as he humours her to a certain extent.

The gesture of Big placing the shoe on Carrie's foot deliberately references Cinderella, a motif that is pursued in the course of the film. Carrie reads Cinderella to Charlotte's daughter earlier on, and in the wake of her breakup advises Lily, 'You know that this is just a fairy tale, sweetheart, and things don't always happen like this in real life. I just think you should know that now.' Yet the film does provide the fairy tale ending, with Big as her Prince Charming who can make her wishes come true, whether they be for a bigger closet or marriage. This is all part of a larger mythical framework for the film, which is typical of the genre, that of belief in the possibility of true love, that this is the Holy Grail that must be pursued by the women. Carrie's assistant, Louise (Jennifer Hudson), hands her talisman, the key ring spelling out 'love', to Carrie when she abandons her career and new life in New York in order to return home to be with her man.

Samantha stands out as being a very different representation of femininity; she is older, egocentric and opinionated, yet ultimately a feminist role model. The film concludes with Samantha choosing to be single again, rejecting her doting, 'toy boy' actor boyfriend. Her choice is a defiant statement of independence and confidence as she returns to New York to resume her life with her friends. This is celebrated in the final scene as Samantha, ' … fifty and fabulous', is toasted by Carrie; she is a positive role model in terms of making her own choices and welcoming the freedom of being single, her vitality and forceful character reversing the usual stereotype of the sad, middle-aged 'singleton'.

Samantha contrasts with the other women in many ways. She has a voracious sexual appetite, yet does not need men. She resents the compromises of coupled life, preferring to have a little lapdog which can easily be carried around in a handbag. She is powerful and successful in her career, outspoken and loyal in her friendships. Samantha rivals Carrie in the flamboyance of her dress, wearing vivid primary colours, plunging necklines and towering heels. Her femininity is on display, reflecting her extraordinary self-confidence and liberated sexuality.

Samantha's storyline revolves around her decision to finish with her long-standing partner, resenting the role in which she finds herself as his wife in all but name: 'I'm not the type of woman who sits home all day waiting for a man!' Samantha rejects the conventional in not conforming to what women are supposed to want; she asserts her independence defiantly when breaking the news to Smith: ' ... I love you. It's just ... I'm just going to say the thing you're not supposed to say. I love you, but I love me more. I've been in a relationship with myself for forty nine years, and that's the one I need to work on.' She has to break free, as she is stifled and unhappy in the relationship, yet Smith is a Hollywood hunk who adores her. The gender roles are reversed in their relationship: he remembers their anniversary, she's oblivious; he turns down the sex she wants, as he needs to get to bed; he buys her the expensive ring she wanted, she is annoyed because she wanted to buy it for herself and is concerned that he might intend it as an engagement ring.

Samantha is a woman who is so empowered that her key characteristic is one that is more masculine than feminine, a fear of monogamy and a desire for sex without strings. Her priority is self-gratification, touching on a vital aspect of the post-feminist zeitgeist of the 'because I'm worth it' generation. The movie as a whole purveys an ambivalent ideology; on the one hand a woman can be successful at work and at play, and hence is entitled to rewards and rights, such as the right to self-gratification, yet on the other hand, as we see with Miranda and Carrie, there is a very traditional message that women should not be *too* self-indulgent, and need to consider others first. In some respects Samantha's character can be traced back to the heroine of the screwball comedy: she is feisty and wilful, exuberant and energetic, unpredictable and capable of creating chaos in the man's world. It is ironic that the older woman in the narrative makes the choices that the younger romcom heroine, in this case Carrie, is not yet ready to make. Indeed it may be argued that Carrie settles for the Wrong Man, the man who is the perennial source of suffering and tears, and who ultimately promises to perpetuate the narrative.

3

THE HERO OF THE ROMANTIC COMEDY

The male hero is at the heart of the romcom, needing to be a plausible object of desire for the woman, and for the audience. He must be our fantasy and offer the heroine what she lacks. On close inspection, certain elements of the male hero are repeated across the decades, suggesting that maybe the representation of gender in this genre is slow to change, if at all. In many romantic comedies the hero is a catalyst for the heroine, propelling her into a journey involving difficult lessons and emotional growth, with the ultimate reward of future mutual happiness, as in It Happened One Night. Commonly the hero is the adversary for the heroine, challenging her values and even her lifestyle, yet the conflict is inevitably founded on a mutual attraction, as is evident in films such as the sex comedies.

THE SCREWBALL HERO

The romantic comedy in its earliest significant cycle, the screwball comedy, can be seen as a response to changing attitudes towards relationships and gender in the early twentieth century, yet many aspects of the representation of femininity seem prescient and radical. The screwball male tends to fall into two main types: the innocent and the father figure. Characters such as Godfrey in *My Man Godfrey* and Peter Warne in *It Happened One Night* offer benevolent paternal guidance to the spoilt heiresses who have lost their way in life. Whereas Professor David Huxley (*Bringing Up Baby*), 'Hopsie' Pike (*The Lady Eve*) and Jerry Warriner (*The Awful Truth*) offer a different hero, the naive innocent who needs to be guided by a woman in order to find happiness. Yet in turn all of these men have lost their way and need to be transformed by love into fully functioning, emotionally intelligent adults. This theme recurs throughout the history of the romcom, lying at the very heart of the contemporary romcom, especially in the male-centred comedies such as *Knocked Up* and *The 40 Year Old Virgin*. Here the central characters are in a state of arrested development, living as perpetual children, being unable to embrace adulthood.

Peter Warne is a drunk and jobless journalist, and Godfrey is a down and out living on the city dump. Both conform to the archetype of the masterful male, but have their own inadequacies and weaknesses to wrestle with. We can read their characters as being symptomatic of the general collapse of certainties in 1930s America, where patriarchy has failed and society is being tested. The need to find a sense of identity and purpose, to restore the familial structures, drives the ideology of these films. Yet the films also provide a sense of release and fun, deliberately inverting the known and familiar, just to restore the equilibrium at the end, with the couple being established, the 'right' man united with the heroine.

The innocence of the later screwball comedies marks a maturing of the genre, contemporaneous with the recovery from the worst of the Depression, the economic slump that dominated the 1930s. The hero is no longer masterful, needing to mature and embrace his masculinity, the heroine being the catalyst for this emotional journey. As we saw with *Bringing Up Baby*, David is emasculated by his fiancée, Susan crashes into his life and forces him out of his museum, out into the world. She creates a series of testing situations and destroys his work, literally demolishing the brontosaurus skeleton he's been working on for years. David has to be railroaded into acting on his feelings, much in the same way as Hopsie proves himself so easily led in *The Lady Eve*.

Hopsie has taken refuge from the modern world, exiling himself into the jungle and the study of snakes; he is clearly ill at ease in society and needs to take refuge from social interaction. Hopsie earnestly assures the Professor on leaving the Amazon that, had he his own way, he would spend all his time on such expeditions, 'in the company of men like yourselves and in the pursuit of knowledge'. Comedy is created from this social awkwardness as girls try to attract the attention of the tycoon's son on the ship, yet he hides behind his book, *Are Snakes Necessary?* The title of the book clearly suggests an apt innuendo, as Hopsie suppresses his masculinity, only to lose control on meeting Jean Harrington (Barbara Stanwyck), whereupon he temporarily loses the snake he has been entrusted with. It is made clear that Hopsie lives in the shadow of his wealthy father, who has funded the expedition, indulging his son's interests, again making clear that he has been emasculated. Kendall points out that Hopsie 'isn't just a caricature of youthful masculinity, he's also an embodiment of Sturges's idea of excessive wealth' (1990: 250). The film is typical of the screwball in providing a critique of the rich, exploring how wealth can be a barrier to emotional intelligence and happiness.

The final scene of *The Lady Eve* sees Hopsie grabbing Jean and leading her to a cabin, striding with purpose and urgency in order to consummate their relationship. He is now transformed, having been empowered as a result of Jean's machinations. He has become the man she wanted him to be, no longer being helpless when confronted with the opposite sex, but ready to take charge and initiate. As is expected of the romcom, order is restored at the conclusion of the narrative, having been inverted as gender differences have been blurred and manliness lost, then found again.

THE CONTEMPORARY HERO

A similar hero can be found in the contemporary romcom, albeit within a rather different social context. In *Failure To Launch*, Tripp (Matthew McConaughey), like Hopsie, is still living at home with his parents, much to their frustration. His character represents a new generation of single men who are reluctant to take on responsibility and commitment, presenting a threat to the continuity of society. Typically, romantic comedies are about reconciliation and restoration of order within relationships and society as a whole. Paula (Sarah Jessica Parker) has created a profession out of re-educating these men, by taking them through a sequence of steps to reintegrate into society, and ultimately to get them to leave the 'nest'. Tripp spends all his spare time with his friends, pursuing their boyish hobbies, much as Hopsie has taken refuge in the world of snakes. A running joke emphasises how unnatural this lifestyle is, as Tripp is recurrently attacked by nature itself, being bitten by a chipmunk, a dolphin and a lizard.

Diane Negra points out how the film is typical of contemporary popular culture in recurrent representations of 'deficient/dysfunctional single masculinity' (2006: 1). Such representations seem to be a response to media concern about the underachievement of men in education, as they are often seen to be left behind as women grasp career opportunities and postpone commitment. This particular character type lies at the heart of what Jeffers McDonald labels the 'hommecom' (2007: 108), that is, the male-centred romantic comedy with a hero who has failed to effect the transition into manhood, living in a state of arrested development. Judd Apatow's comedies are defined by this particular phenomenon, repositioning the genre to appeal to a broader male audience, with positive representations of male bonding and sympathetic male characters who support the hero. The payoff for such a shift in the centre of gravity within the genre is correspondingly negative representations of women, as they are seen as 'other' to the hero, and within the narrative. The woman can be a threat, cynical and calculating, or even someone who is mysterious and unknowable, reinforcing the stereotype of the irrationality of women. Despite the relevance of such gender representations to a Western society that has soaring numbers of single households and plunging marriage rates, these representations are still familiar from earlier romantic comedies, building on perennial gender stereotypes.

Towards the end of *Failure To Launch*, our position regarding Tripp is radically challenged as it is revealed that in actual fact his desperate pursuit of boyish pleasures is a reaction to the death of his former girlfriend; instead of seeming irresponsible and ridiculous, his behaviour arouses pathos and he gains our sympathy. Paula's vocation in seeking to kick-start such slackers suddenly seems even more cynical and irresponsible, let alone morally reprehensible. This is typical of what Kathleen Rowe identifies in the 'postclassical' romantic comedy, that is the 'melodramatised man' who appropriates stereotypically feminine character traits, seeming to break with more traditional representations of men as emotionally repressed. Rowe asserts that actually such representations serve to reinforce the patriarchy, as the hero becomes empowered by moral superiority and sensitivity, able to '"instruct" women about relationships, romance and femininity itself' (1995: 196–97). Our sympathies are engaged for Tripp, and Paula is forced to learn a painful lesson as a result of his suffering. In 27 Dresses, Kevin (James Marsden) helps to release Jane (Katherine Heigl) from her life's miserable stalemate by counselling her as to how to assert herself, as she continually subjugates herself to the wishes of others. His advice is the catalyst to her gaining greater self-knowledge and they are both rewarded through marriage to each other. Kevin is represented as a sensitive and supportive proposition, albeit rather cynical on the surface, as a result of the hurt from his failed marriage. He is a variation of the melodramatised man who 'instructs' and 'educates' the heroine in order to effect her transformation. Jane is a veritable Cinderella, who lacks the strength to release herself from her prison. She refuses to acknowledge Kevin's advances, as she is frozen in a pathological stupor, whereas Kevin reinforces his paternal role in facilitating her escape. The extent of Jane's empowerment is only to enable her to choose him over her boss, promoting her from the role of bridesmaid to that of bride.

THE PLAYBOY

One of the perennial problems facing the romcom hero is the conflict between the pleasures of the bachelor lifestyle and the often dubious advantages of married life. The hero of the screwball genre is clearly living an incomplete life without another half, yet since that era it is not always absolutely clear what is to be gained from married life, for the man in particular. There are some notable exceptions to this: Spencer Tracy and Katharine Hepburn need to be together, the conflict between them being an essential part of their relationship in *Adam's Rib*. The essential paradox at the heart of the nervousness of Woody Allen's comedies is that he cannot function without his partner, yet cannot function with a partner either.

The 1950s was a time for renewed emphasis on traditional gender roles, with Cold War role models such as John Wayne asserting a very macho masculinity. The bachelor playboy of the sex comedies of the late 1950s and early 1960s is a problematic figure within this context. He is very assured in his sexuality, and is the envy of other men for his success with the other sex, yet he is not conforming with the social norms of the time, being a bachelor and consequently childless. The playboy is a threat to social equilibrium, who needs to be cut down to size and integrated into society. He is a fantasy figure, with his enviable lifestyle and dedication to pleasure, yet the audience can feel gratification, as the playboy is normalised at the end of the film, with marriage and children. This character type defined Rock Hudson's film roles at this time in his pairing with Doris Day. Hudson's character in films such as *Pillow Talk* and *Lover Come Back* is seen to lead a glamorous and enviable lifestyle, with an endless string of lithe young women queuing up to be with him. He is a successful figure who lives in a sumptuous bachelor pad with all the accoutrements to impress ... and seduce. A recurring joke in *Lover Come Back* has two older men happening upon Jerry Webster in various compromising positions and being deeply astounded, and impressed, by his virility. Jerry is the archetypal sex comedy hero, in that he is motivated by the desire for sex but needs to learn the value of commitment and love.

Jerry does not seem to suffer for the excessive pleasures of his lifestyle: he is popular and successful. This character is actually deeply opposed to marriage, seeing it as a threat to his freedom and happiness.

In *Pillow Talk* Brad declaims: 'Before a man gets married he's like a tree in the forest ... And then the tree gets cut down ... thrown in the river ... taken to the mill and when it comes out it's no longer a tree, it's the vanity table, the breakfast nook, the baby crib and the newspaper that lines the family garbage can!' Brad's fear of marriage is corrected in the course of the narrative, through the process of emotional education that is typical of the genre. His friend, Jonathan, counters his fears by explaining, 'That's what it means to be adult. A wife, a family, a house. A mature man wants those responsibilities.' The playboy is a boy who needs to develop the maturity to be a worthy partner for the ultimate prize, the 'good' girl: Doris Day. The film shows that commitment can enhance your manliness as Brad concludes it by bursting into Jan's apartment and carrying her across town to his place, in a display of macho strength and authority.

Figure 3.1 Brad becomes masterful in *Pillow Talk*.

For a female audience, Brad is a desirable figure, an attractive and sexually experienced man who is clearly adept when it comes to women. He lives a fantasy lifestyle, but he is also a threat, as he is clearly promiscuous. The audience can be gratified, as Brad is made into an attainable figure if he can fall in love with the girl-next-door type and remain virile, yet monogamous. He is contained and integrated into society through marriage and commitment.

The same transformation of the playboy can be found in contemporary romantic comedies. Ben (Matthew McConaughey) enjoys a life as a successful advertising executive (like Jerry Webster in *Lover Come Back*), with all the accoutrements of the playboy lifestyle, in *How To Lose A Guy In 10 Days*. Much like the Hudson/Day sex comedies, Ben gains maturity and self-knowledge through masquerade as he lies to Andie (Kate Hudson) and conceals his true identity and motives. Initially he is threatened by the incursion of the feminine into his bachelor pad as Andie deliberately parades a parodic excess of femininity in his space with her wedding album, cuddly toys and toiletries. By the end of the film he demonstrates a macho command of the situation, similar to Brad, by pursuing Andie as she leaves for her new job and stopping her taxi.

The romantic comedy hero can also be represented initially as a threat to the heroine by exhibiting an excess of masculinity, and perhaps seeking to limit her potential to succeed, particularly with regard to work and other relationships. With Brad and Ben this manifests itself in the urge to seduce, but without wanting commitment, this being at odds with the interests and well-being of the heroine. Sex here is a threat, as it is purely about male gratification and self-interest. Kevin (Tom Hanks) in *You've Got Mail* is a smart business man whose flourishing bookshop chain leads to the demise of Kathleen's (Meg Ryan) small independent bookshop. His aggressive and ruthless business practices allow no room for the quirky individualism and warmth of his competitor, and he destroys her livelihood. Hildy divorces Walter in *His Girl Friday* because he neglected her for his work, only to find that he is prepared to go to any lengths to wreck her chances of marrying again because he is determined that she should be his. Nevertheless, Hildy gives in to Walter, realising that she loves him and he is right in asserting that she would be bored with another; his power and determination are irresistible. Yet generally, the process of transformation and education leads to the couples learning from each other and masculinity is tempered by love, the threat being transformed into harmonious union. Kathleen has inadvertently befriended the other side to Kevin: unbeknownst to them both, he has been her penpal confidante with whom she has shared her fears and experiences. He has proved himself as a worthy partner in giving her sensitive advice and emotional support, being more of a 'new man', the man who is in touch with his feminine side.

CASE STUDY: *IT HAPPENED ONE NIGHT*

It Happened One Night was an enormous hit for Columbia Studios, which was not one of the major Hollywood studios, having a reputation for small-budget films, even needing to borrow its stars from other studios. The film was the first to win all five of the Academy Awards for which it was nominated, an event that has only occurred a couple times since: Best Director, Best Actor, Best Actress, Best Film and Best Writing. The director, Frank Capra, had developed his reputation with a series of romances in the late 1920s and early 1930s, helping to keep the studio profitable during the Depression.

It Happened One Night was a seminal film, being widely recognised as the first screwball comedy, having the unique approach of casting two central stars, male and female, who are simultaneously the romantic and the comic leads. In terms of screwball conventions we have the warring couple, from contrasting social backgrounds, who start in a state of antipathy to each other but end up falling in love. The plot features masquerades, a runaway bride, a race against time, romantic interludes and misunderstandings. Ellie Andrews (Claudette Colbert) has married celebrity aviator King Westley (Jameson Thomas), but her father disapproves of her choice and seeks to annul the marriage, keeping her prisoner on his yacht in Miami. Ellie decides to escape and join Westley in New York. She throws herself overboard, swims to shore and then manages to get a bus ticket to New York. On the bus she meets Peter Warne (Clark Gable), who has just been sacked from his newspaper job. He ends up assisting her in getting to New York, despite their clashing personalities. They proceed to fall in love, only for misunderstanding to result in Ellie being on the verge of properly marrying Westley. Her father collaborates in helping Ellie run away – for the second time – from the wedding ceremony, to drive away with Peter. The film merges the morphology of the fairy tale with the energy and playfulness of a comedy, allowing for an exploration of romance and relationships. It was a creative landmark, incorporating Capra's concerns with class and wealth, the independent woman and the power of love 'to transcend social boundaries' (Kendall, 1990: 32).

Ellie is the spoilt and bored heiress, trying to escape from the authority of her father, whilst Peter is the rather dissolute journalist who has just been sacked from his paper. Ellie is very much the archetype of the screwball heroine, as discussed in the previous chapter. She is feisty and unpredictable, determined to do things her way and capable of giving as good as she gets with her sharp repartee. She shows a radical disrespect for rules and authority, relishing the opportunity to assert her will and to break away from convention. Yet the edicts of the screwball comedy stipulate that Ellie needs to meet her match and that she needs a man who is her equal in vitality and adventurousness, but who can also contain and 'educate' her.

Clark Gable was an established Hollywood star by the time he came to the film, but this was his first comic role. One story suggests that he was sent to Columbia on loan as punishment by MGM for asking for a pay rise, and that he was drunk when he first reported to the studio. Gable brought to the role of Peter Warne this reputation for mischief, but also a debonair self-assurance that had distinguished his performances, especially as a romantic lead. Capra was looking for a romantic hero who was a man of the people and who represented the values and character that an American public, suffering the rigours of the

Depression, would respect and aspire towards. Peter Warne is a plain-speaking everyman who brooks no nonsense from anyone, be it a tycoon or a bus driver. He is resourceful and independent, able to survive with nothing to his name, by eating carrots, making a bed out of straw and using his thumb to get around. He is reduced to having nothing more than the clothes on his back, much like the worst casualties of the economic collapse, yet he is not a man just to sit back and accept whatever fate throws at him. When the only seat on the bus is used to transport papers, he just throws them out of the window; when a crook tries to drive off with Peter's case, Peter runs after the car, catches up with it, gives the driver a beating, and then drives the car away himself; and when Ellie seems to have abandoned him for King Westley, he demands back the expenses that he incurred in looking after her.

Capra deliberately made the hero a working man, in contrast to the original story on which he based the script, where the hero was a penniless inventor from a wealthy background. Peter's status is made clear, for example, when he drives his beat-up old car along the dusty roads in the early morning to get back to Ellie, contrasted with the slick comfort of the capacious automobile carrying Ellie's father and King Westley, which speeds its way past him, accompanied by a noisy police escort. Peter is at home out on the road, waving at the hobos on the train, whistling with the birds and bantering with the level-crossing man. The audience sympathise with him as his car fails to keep up with the cavalcade as he tries to get to Ellie, the hopelessness of his situation highlighted by the close-up of his tyre deflating.

The mode of transport defines the man, as Peter relies on public transport, his thumb and a clapped-out old banger that he 'appropriated' from the scoundrel who tried to steal his case. This is in contrast to Ellie's 'husband', King Westley, a celebrity aviator, who turns their wedding into even more of a spectacle by arriving in an autogyro, an extravagant gesture. Westley is a rather restrained, mannered, dark-suited, angular figure, who typically grasps a cane, suggesting sophistication and status. Paradoxically, it is Peter who exudes an adventurous, devil-may-care attitude that one would expect of the aviator; he is loose limbed and jaunty, moving freely whilst grasping a battered suitcase, possessing energy and self-composure. Ellie realises what she wants from life, declaring to Westley as they are about to be married: 'I want our life to be full of excitement, we will never let up will we, never a dull moment. We'll get on a merry-go-round and never get off. Promise you'll never let me get off.' This is what life with Peter was like on the road, and why she ultimately runs away from Westley. We only ever see Westley in confined spaces, indoors, whereas Peter is at ease out in the country, whether it be sleeping under the stars or fording a river. He is the real man, who is at one with nature and can survive hardship, in comparison to the artifice and extravagance of Westley.

Travel is a key theme throughout the film, which in many respects is a road movie, the journey of the characters being metaphorical and emotional as well as physical. The characters are rarely still for long, from the moment Ellie dives off her father's yacht, to the climax, when Ellie clambers into the car to escape her wedding, continuing her journey. The film hinges on the bus journey during which Ellie and Peter get to know each other, the inhabitants of the bus forming a cross-section of the real America that Peter is at home in but that Ellie has never had a chance to experience. They start the journey estranged from each other at the back of the bus, but as time progresses they move into the heart of the bus, and join in the singing as Ellie is integrated into the bus's community.

Peter Warne's character was based on the wise-cracking newshound that was a familiar character type to contemporary audiences, but the fact that he is 'one of us' was important to the theme of social reconciliation. Typically for the screwball comedy, the world of the rich is represented as flawed and self-indulgent, reinforcing the simple message that money does not buy happiness. Peter's role is to stand in stark relief to the values of the rich, to represent the down-to-earth values that would help get the nation back on its feet. Peter wastes no time in confronting Ellie with her shortcomings. He is straight talking, funny and arrogant, taking on the challenge of educating her:

You're just the spoiled brat of a rich father. The only way you get anything is to buy it ... Haven't you ever heard of the word humility? I guess it never occurred to you to say 'please Mister, I'm in trouble, will you help me?' No, that would bring you down off your high horse for a minute.

Ellie is initially enraged by his arrogance and directness, but she learns that he is right, and realigns her values and sense of self by the end of the film. Ultimately she realises that she owes an enormous debt of gratitude to Peter, and that she needs his paternal guidance, as she confesses to her father: 'Peter says that I'm spoiled and selfish and pampered and thoroughly insincere. He doesn't think so much of you either, he blames you for everything that's wrong with me ... .'

Peter is the spokesperson for the common man, he dares to say the unsayable, whether it is in confronting Ellie with some home truths, or insulting his boss. There is no doubt about Peter's sincerity, he is a transparent character who says what he thinks, and to hell with the consequences. He tells Ellie exactly what he thinks of her when she tries to bribe him to help her. The tables are turned as the heiress has to turn to the working man for assistance and finds that money cannot buy you everything. His honesty and abrasiveness are shocking for Ellie, but he is clearly more than a match for her wilful and indulged nature. Peter is her nemesis, who wages his own 'shock and awe' campaign, fulfilling the role of the fierce and uncompromising parent figure. This is shown to be exactly what Ellie needed as she comes to respect and trust Peter, assuming the role of a miscreant daughter who needs firm handling. From the first, Peter addresses her as 'brat', telling her that she is 'as helpless as a baby' and continually putting her in her place. Peter automatically takes the upper hand in their relationship, as she is out of her natural environment and hence dependent on him, having little choice but clearly coming to desire his domineering presence.

Peter commandeers Ellie's world from the first, taking control of everything, from what she eats to how she dresses. He stops her from buying chocolates on the bus, grabbing her purse, counting her money and then pronouncing that she's 'on a budget from now on', telling her to 'shuddup' when she protests. Their relationship instantly assumes a particular hierarchy, with the rich girl being put in her place by the domineering male. To some extent the audience are invited to approve of this, as we see that Ellie is indeed spoilt and arrogant, but the contemporary audience may well have had an even keener interest in the rich being taught a lesson by the common man. Peter is ready to physically enforce his primacy, even if in jest, assuring her father that 'what she needs is a guy that will take a sock at her, once a day, whether she had it coming to her or not'. He smacks her playfully when she boasts of her father's piggybacking prowess. The relationship seems to concur with the social pressure to restore traditional gender roles and family values as Ellie escapes from one oppressive patriarchal regime, with her father, to surrender to another with Peter.

Yet there is somewhat more to Peter than being a father figure to Ellie; he is nurturing and protective, showing maternal traits in giving her a scarf, being concerned about her damp clothes and preparing her breakfast.

Again, he proves himself resourceful, but also caring. He assumes the role of provider in procuring food and bedding, ensuring that one way or another they have transport and somewhere to sleep. Ellie proves herself next to useless, and almost entirely reliant on him; her major contribution is to flash her leg to get a lift for them both. He is also a gentleman, who is respectful of her privacy in hanging the blanket between their beds at the Auto Camp, restraining himself from taking advantage of her vulnerability, despite his obvious feelings of attraction. This was particularly important, given the context of the film, with the enforcement of the Production Code in 1934 and a new mood of restraint and moral sensitivity.

It is made clear that Peter, as a romantic comedy hero, is a figure of desire for Ellie, and for the audience. This is made particularly evident when he strips off in front of Ellie, daring her to stay put and watch, in order to embarrass her and force her to retreat to her bed. The camera stays fixed as, along with Ellie, we gaze at his body until he starts to

Figure 3.2 Peter is nurturing and protective towards Ellie in It *Happened One Night*.

undo his trousers. Peter has charisma, commanding attention wherever he is. When we first meet him at the bus depot he is the centre of attention for a gang of journalists, who hang on his every word and form an unlikely congregation for him as he gets on the bus, declaiming drunkenly 'Make way for the king! Long live the king!' Even his editor is forgiving and tolerant of him, despite his bad behaviour and having fired him previously, thrusting some money into his pocket when he realises how upset Peter is about Ellie's reunion with King Westley.

Peter is a romantic hero as well. We learn, along with Ellie, that he has a softer more vulnerable side and that he has dreams and desires, when she asks him if he has ever been in love. He wants 'someone who is real, someone who is alive ... ' and describes himself as 'a sucker' for making plans for his perfect romance. The camera cuts between a soft-focus close-up of Peter lying in bed, and Ellie, who sits forlornly on her bed, behind the 'Wall of Jericho', as he terms the dividing blanket. He reveals a romanticised image of his perfect relationship, which involves fun and adventure, as well as passion: ' ... nights when you, and the moon, and the surf all become one ... '. His words drive Ellie to declare her feelings to him, as she is unable to resist the future that could be theirs.

Peter is a flawed hero, nevertheless. His first appearance shows him to be drunk and boastful, as well as argumentative, yet his jaunty demeanour and mischievous face exonerate him, as does his obvious popularity. His behaviour towards Ellie is rude and overbearing, yet she is equally contemptuous to start with. As with any screwball hero, we see Peter learning from Ellie, much as she is 'educated' by him. She provides an outlet for his adventurous and romantic nature, teaching him about love. Nevertheless, he has changed little by the end of the film, whereas Ellie has chosen to leave behind the glamour of her potential life with Westley, as well as having grown up in the course of her journey with Peter. The final shot of the auto camp cabin signifies the nature of their life together; it will be on his terms, and in his world, the world of the ordinary American.

It Happened One Night is very much a fairy tale on the surface, where the princess is rescued by a dashing prince from her fate out in the wilderness. The prince is fearless and protects the princess from any threats (the lascivious salesman on the bus), overcoming obstacles to help her escape. The princess's father grants his permission for her to marry the prince and they live happily ever after. Yet this is a fairy tale that is set against the backdrop of social inequality and deprivation, where the characters are flawed and are very much opposites in many ways. Their characters reveal much about contemporary attitudes to gender and relationships.

CASE STUDY: *KNOCKED UP*

Knocked Up marked a distinctive new departure for the romantic comedy, following on from the success of The 40 Year Old Virgin, borrowing extensively from the gross-out comedies of the past decade and appealing to a broader audience as a consequence. Both films were written and directed by Judd Apatow. Apatow is very much an auteur, working with a particular group of actors and writers, producing films that deal with representations of men in crisis, purveying 'the kind of conservative morals the Family Research Council might embrace – if the humor weren't so filthy' (Rodrick, 2007). The film met with general critical approval, an unusual situation for a romantic comedy, perhaps reflecting its appeal to a male audience. Nevertheless, since its release there has been much debate about the gender representations in the film, with accusations of sexism, partly as a result of the comments of the film's female star, Katherine Heigl.

The narrative brings together attractive, successful TV presenter Alison Scott (Heigl) and a dope-smoking, unemployed, chubby slacker, Ben Stone (Seth Rogen), who, after a one-night stand, find that Alison is pregnant. After the initial shock, Ben supports her in keeping the baby and they decide to try to make a go of it together. Alison realises that she doesn't believe that Ben is committed enough and dumps him, but when she goes into labour she turns to him for help, and they finish the film together as happy parents. At the same time, Alison's sister, Debbie, and her husband, Pete, are going through a crisis in their marriage, breaking up and then getting back together again.

The seeming incompatibility of the central couple is typical of the romantic comedy, with the pairing of the well-favoured heroine with the less illustrious male. This is essentially a similar situation to many classic romcom couples, such as in *Bringing Up Baby* and *It Happened One Night*. *Knocked Up* presents us with a couple who are very much of the 21st century in terms of struggling to find a way forward, reconciling the expectations of friends, family, career (for Alison) and society. They don't know what decisions to make or how to be adults, veering from one stressful situation to the next. For both characters, male and female, there is a shortage of responsible role models. Alison's mother proves herself cold and unfeeling in bluntly telling Alison that she

Figure 3.3 The mismatched couple in *Knocked Up*.

should have an abortion, and her sister is a neurotic control freak. Ben's father is bemused that Ben should ask him for advice, not seeing himself as any kind of role model:

MR STONE: Ben, I've been divorced three times, why would you listen to me?
BEN: Because you were the only one giving me advice, and it was terrible advice.
MR STONE: You can go round blaming everyone else, but in the end, until you start taking responsibility for yourself, none of this is going to work out.
BEN: I don't know how to take responsibility for myself ... I'm an idiot, just tell me what to do!

Nevertheless Ben's father does prove to be a positive role model for Ben. They are very similar characters, as is highlighted by their appearance as they sit opposite each other in the restaurant while Ben tells his father about the pregnancy. His father is warm and supportive, assuring Ben that he 'was the best thing that ever happened' to him and gently teasing him when Ben talks of his 'vision' of how his life would go. When Ben worries about his drug use and the baby, it transpires that his father was a pot head too, reinforcing the fact that they are kindred spirits. His father's enthusiasm and laid-back attitude stands in stark relief to the horror exhibited by Alison's mother. Stereotypical expectations of gender are reversed here, as the mother is unsympathetic and more concerned about Alison's career, whereas Ben's father is excited about the baby, showing a warmth and humanity that are very much part of his son.

Ben conforms to the boy/man archetype that is often to be found in contemporary romcoms. He lives a carefree, hedonistic life, firmly ensconced within a group of like-minded friends with whom he lives and plays. The opening montage quickly outlines what we should know about him as we see him playing with his friends, in a sequence of comic scenarios: fighting with boxing gloves on fire, being scared on a roller-coaster and smoking grass inside a weird goldfish-bowl contraption. Play and self-gratification are clearly of central importance in their lives. The 'boys' are sympathetically represented as lovable slackers, happy in their own carefree world. Their attempt at making a living consists of setting up a website, 'fleshofthestars.com', featuring clips of female nudity from the movies. Being such slackers, they have not done their research, discovering later on that such a site already exists. The scenes featuring Ben and his friends are characterised by a warm, male camaraderie, but also the gross-out style of humour that further accentuates their comic immaturity. Apatow commented on this phenomenon: 'I don't imagine that American men ever found it easy to grow up … But now you can delay it your whole life' (Hiatt, 2007). This attitude provides the bedrock for many contemporary representations of Western masculinity.

The film frequently cuts from scenes featuring Ben and his friends, to scenes in Debbie and Pete's household, serving to highlight the tension and unhappiness to be found in their marriage, in contrast to the relaxed buffoonery to be found in Ben's household. Debbie's face is strained and rigid, as is her body language, as she continually fights to get what she wants in her marriage. She is relentless in trying to whip Pete into shape, coming across as a harridan. Inevitably this creates a very negative representation of marriage, making the slacker lifestyle seem appealing in its irresponsible self-indulgence. As Pete confides to Ben: 'Marriage is like an unfunny, tense version of Everybody Loves Raymond, but it doesn't last twenty two minutes, it lasts forever.'

Ben is far from the typical romcom hero in his looks, being more reminiscent of Woody Allen in having an unconventional look. He is not unlike a man-sized cherub: chubby, baby faced and curly haired, with a benevolent yet mischievous demeanour. His pudginess is part of his childlike character, as is made manifest as he plays with Alison's nieces. Ben is jammed in their playhouse, creating an incongruous image as he chats about grass with the children, and then has difficulty extracting himself from the house. This reinforces the essential ingenuousness of Ben's character; the immaturity of his slacker lifestyle is actually a redeeming factor, as he knows how to play and be happy. As far back as the screwball comedies, a common theme has been the importance of play in forging a healthy relationship between the central couple. Ben knows how to play and understands its importance, in contrast to Pete, who muses as to why children like bubbles so much. Ben understands the appeal of bubbles:

BEN: They float; you can pop 'em. I get it, I get it.
PETE: I wish I liked anything as much as my kids like bubbles.
BEN: That's sad.
PETE: It's totally sad. Their smiling faces point out your inability to enjoy anything.

Pete and Debbie's relationship is a warning about how restricting and soul-destroying marriage can be. Pete no longer knows how to be happy, yet he and Debbie have the perfect life on the surface. Pete is successful in his career; they are both attractive and have two healthy children and a lovely house. Ben is a chubby slacker who can barely afford to buy spaghetti, as Alison points out, and lives in a messy, shared house.

The physical disparity between him and Alison is not lost on Ben as he informs her, in wonder, 'You're prettier than I am'. Alison is disgusted by the reality of Ben the morning after they have had sex; she cannot bear to go near him, prodding at the bed with her foot. Apatow highlights the differences between the couple as they leave Alison's room: Alison is in a chic suit and high heels, ready for work in her new job at the TV station, whilst Ben ambles along in his grungy T-shirt and jeans, having no particular work to go to, and then proceeding to 'yak up' at the diner, much to Alison's disgust.

Yet Ben endears himself to the audience, as he is clearly aware of how Alison feels about him and has no delusions about himself. He lacks self-confidence, and proves himself vulnerable, having clearly suffered from rejection in the past. When Alison asks Ben for reassurance about his commitment he assures her, half in jest, 'I'm the guy girls fuck over ... so you don't fuck me over, okay? I couldn't take it. I can't raise this baby alone.' After his first night with Alison he confides to his housemates, 'She was totally repulsed by me. She didn't even seem to like me ... '. Ben's friends are more than his playmates, as he is able to confide in them and even seeks their advice and support at critical times. They rush to the hospital to support him when the baby arrives, sharing in his anguish and joy, declaring 'We're having a baby', as if they are all fathers to the child. It is a positive representation of male camaraderie, presenting the male characters as being sensitive and emotional. Nevertheless, there is a sense of naivety and immaturity regarding their understanding of women. Women are clearly regarded as sex objects by the household, as is indicated by their website – they are incredulous that Alison does not find it appealing. Ben is also an object of admiration for his friends as a result of sleeping with Alison: 'I think it's awesome that you had sex with her. If a goofy guy like you had sex with her, I feel like I had sex with her also.' Alison represents a fantasy ideal of womanhood for them, with her glossy, blonde good looks; she is an image of feminine perfection, which clearly remains out of reach for the slacker household.

Apatow's movies explore a common theme, seeing the underdog, the male underachiever managing to achieve credibility through partnership with beauty. The prince, in these romances, does not have the aesthetic appeal of the traditional hero, yet he is rewarded for his essential goodness with the princess. Apatow's movies are directed more at a male audience, giving them the opportunity to identify with the flawed hero. Some commentators have decried this particular trend in the romantic comedy, as Anne Billson pleads, 'I'm fed up with charmless slackers like Seth Rogen getting off with hotties, so how about a romcom about a girl geek who gets knocked up by an overachieving Mr McDreamy?' (Billson, 2009). Kira Cochrane has written about her unease at seeing successful female characters being reduced in status by being paired with inadequates, as if to redress the gender power balance.

Knocked Up remains true to the romantic comedy formula in having the central couple learn from each other, their relationship progressing through the challenges posed by their very different characters and attitudes. Much of the essential comedy of the narrative is based on the seemingly irreconcilable differences between the two, both physically and in terms of their lifestyles. The baby is what yokes them together as they try to make a go of it early on in the film, despite the initial repugnance that Alison feels towards Ben. He has to undergo a process of transformation in order to be worthy of Alison and the baby. Ben enters into Alison's world, embracing the activities she initiates, going to the gynaecologist, shopping for baby books and equipment and spending time with her family. Again, the audience are positioned to be sympathetic to Ben's plight as he struggles to come to terms with the change in his world, having to become a mature and responsible individual, admitting that 'I've only just got used to the notion that someone would have sex with me'. He does everything he can to be supportive, telling Alison, 'I know my job is just to support you in whatever it is you want to do … I'm on board … maybe you could help me, by telling me one thing that I am supposed to do … I really have no idea whatsoever … '.

Alison's fears about Ben and his ability to be a responsible parent are confirmed by the evidence that falls out of his cupboards during the earth tremor. She picks through his possessions, looking despairingly at the evidence of his unsuitability: the cannabis plant, the bank statement making clear his lack of money, the ninja sword and the bag of untouched baby books. In the wake of Alison's rejection, Ben attempts to become the man that she wants; he reads the baby books, buys baby clothes, gets a job and a flat, and makes a home for the new baby. Ben is the new man, he is prepared to take on responsibility and provide for his family, yet he is also sentimental and emotional, embracing fatherhood and demonstrating sensitivity. He puts Alison's needs before his own, ensuring that she gets what she wants even though her demands are seen to be irrational and hysterical when she is in labour. His metamorphosis is complete when he becomes masterful. Debbie tells him to leave when she arrives at the birthing suite, but Ben finally asserts himself with her, telling her to leave. Debbie admires him for this, declaring that she thinks 'he's gonna be a good dad'. She is astonished when he stands up to her, but clearly impressed. He demonstrates the potential to be manly and commanding, unlike her husband, Pete.

Ben is transformed by gaining maturity and responsibility, but it is also clear that he retains his ability to play and have fun. Nevertheless, Alison moves into his world, as is made clear in the final frames as they drive back to the home that Ben has made for them all. Alison does not undergo as fundamental a transformation as Ben in the narrative, yet she does learn to value what Ben represents and espouses his lifestyle and attitudes to some extent. She quickly accepts his friends, even helping out with the research for their website, and she defends Ben in the face of her sister's criticism. Alison has to learn that Ben is the right man for her, and finally realises this when Ben takes control when she is in labour.

The film offers a model for a happy couple, which is much the same as many romcom pairings in suggesting that play and mutual respect are an important basis for success. The film presents a positive representation of male camaraderie, as Ben is supported by his friends and father and, in turn, supports Pete when he is in need. Alison, in contrast is very isolated, only having her sister to turn to, who herself provides a poor role model in her marriage with Pete. Debbie lives by certain rules in her marriage, advising Alison that she needs to 'train' Ben by 'criticising [him] a lot, so that [he] gets so down on himself, that he is forced to change'. Heigl invoked controversy when she criticised the film, saying in *Vanity Fair* that 'It paints the women as shrews, as humourless and uptight, and it paints the men as goofy, fun-loving guys.'

The film endorses the underdog, the underachieving male, suggesting that such a type has important characteristics that the successful woman needs in order to attain happiness. By making Alison pregnant, Ben effectively binds her to him, even though he blames her for the conception, as he naively assumed that she was in charge of the contraception.

4

THE COMEDY OF ROMANCE

The romantic comedy genre is differentiated from the romance and the melodrama by its emphasis on the generation of laughter, placing it firmly within the wider, rather amorphous comedy genre. Comedy is amorphous in covering such a diverse range of forms, ranging from the romantic comedy, through parody and satire, to slapstick. The romantic comedy has established its own narratives and comic language, which clearly define its genre identity. Nevertheless, there are pertinent issues concerning the nature and purpose of the comedy, the positioning of the spectator, and the ideologies that are explored through humour.

The *Collins English Dictionary* defines comedy as 'a film … intended to arouse laughter' and as 'a humorous or satirical play in which the characters ultimately triumph over adversity'. The romantic comedy locates the 'adversity' within the realm of relationships and follows a highly predictable narrative path, leading to the 'triumph' of the happy ending, which sees the couple united as they overcome adversity. The Greek philosopher Aristotle established the fundamental characteristics of comedy in outlining its difference to tragedy. The tragedy leads to an unhappy ending for its protagonist, who is generally of noble origin, whereas comedy represents the lives of those from lower echelons of society and will always lead to a happy ending. The romantic comedy is

seen as being strongly based on the New Comedy tradition, as identified by Northrop Frye, which features a hero from an ordinary background who is in conflict with an older, authoritarian figure. The hero
is hindered in attaining his desires by forces in control of society, yet
the plot sees a reversal of fortune leading to wealth and/or respectability and a new society is formed around the hero and his bride
(1990: 163). Glitre (2006: 12–13) makes a strong case that the Hollywood romantic comedy is not simply based on the New Comedy tradition, in that it foregrounds the woman in the plot, her desires and
actions being as important as, or even more important than, the male's.
She relates it more to the 'battling sexes tradition of Shakespearean
comedy (*The Taming Of The Shrew, Much Ado About Nothing, A Midsummer Night's
Dream*)', but noting that romantic comedy can be shown to have
'multiple and diverse antecedents'.

Kathleen Rowe demonstrates how Northrop Frye's work on the
'utopian dimension' of comedy is useful in understanding how the
romantic comedy 'reworks a common story of community, struggle and
renewal', but in common with other comedies has an emphasis on
renewal (1995: 47). Renewal manifests itself in the renewed commitment to relationships, in the case of reaffirmation comedies such as *His
Girl Friday* or *Four Christmases*, where the main couple get back together
again (Stanley Cavell, 1981, referred to these as 'comedies of remarriage'). Rowe goes on to explain that the comedy revolves around
liberation from 'a world wilting under repressive law … through a
temporary movement into a dimension [of] the carnivalesque … of
festivity and natural regeneration'. The romantic comedy is about the
celebration of love and relationships, lifting the central characters out of
the tedium and loneliness of their normality.

DISPLACEMENT AND DISRUPTION

Geoff King (2002: 5) outlines the conventions of comedy as hinging
on 'departures of a particular kind from what are considered to be

the normal routines of life', the comic impact of which is created through:

- difference from what is usually expected in the non-comic world
- incongruity
- exaggeration
- displacement; sense of things being out of place, mixed up or not quite right.

In Notting Hill, William's life as a lonely, divorced owner of a Notting Hill bookshop is disrupted by Anna, the Hollywood movie star, plunging him into a very different world, that of celebrity and its attendant glamour and press intrusion. Humour is created from the collision between the two worlds, and the many incongruous situations that arise, the impact of which is enhanced by the audience's awareness of the real-life star status of Hugh Grant in the role of William. He is repeatedly shown as being completely out of place in Anna's world, as he is humiliated when visiting her on set and gets mistaken for a journalist when visiting her at The Ritz. The comic tone is heightened by the incongruity of situations such as William's sister surprising the Hollywood star whilst Anna is in the toilet, and when the dishevelled Spike faces the paparazzi in nothing more than his grubby Y-fronts. The comedy is created by a clash of values and culture, which is exaggerated to maximise the sense of displacement and departure that is typical of the romantic comedy.

Social displacement was a popular source of humour in the screwball comedies, such as My Man Godfrey and It Happened One Night. In these films the couple come from contrasting social milieus, creating comedy through the clash of values and lifestyles, yet clearly having an added resonance with a mass audience coming out of the worst of the Great Depression in representing the upper classes as flawed. The displacement can become part of the destabilising process which challenges the couple, encouraging them to revise their priorities and worldview, ultimately leading to recognition of love and the gaining of happiness.

As seen in the previous chapter, romantic comedies often take the couple out of the comforts of their normal environment and into a challenging space, creating a comic sense of dislocation and ensuing incongruities. The 2008 comedy of remarriage *Four Christmases* concerns a happily unmarried couple who live a blissful, affluent lifestyle well away from their embarrassing families. The couple are forced to spend Christmas together with their respective divorced parents, resulting for the first time in a real test of their relationship. They are taken out of their comfort zone as they confront the quirkiness of their eccentric families, whether it is the mother who boasts of her voracious sex life with her son's former best friend, or Brad's (Vince Vaughan) brothers who are hefty, semi-professional, extreme cage fighters. Yet despite the angst and suffering that ensues as they try to deal with the multifarious humiliations and difficulties, the couple end by deciding to start a family themselves, having learned together about the value of family bonds. The couple go through the comic process of displacement, resulting in destabilisation, leading to a stronger bond and even great happiness, as is the typical transformation accomplished by the comedy of remarriage.

Comedy is also about disruption. For the romantic comedy, the disruption may be created from the conflict between the couple, or from the effect of one half of the couple on the life of the other. *Bringing Up Baby*'s comedy arises from the impact of the determined and unfettered Susan (Katharine Hepburn) on David (Cary Grant), with his dry, scholarly existence. Indeed, a central convention of the screwball comedy is this anarchic disruption of the norm, manifested in an exhilarating rush of verbal wit and slapstick comedy, the chemistry between the couple having been the catalyst for this comic abundance. King (2002: 7) notes that 'One of the pleasures offered by comedy is the freedom vicariously to enjoy departures from the norm', yet these departures and disruptions are not meant to be taken too seriously. The spectator watches and enjoys with the reassurance of the genre's safety net, that there will be a happy ending. This marks one of the main differences between the romantic comedy and the romance/melodrama; the pathos of the latter is rarely dissipated by laughter, suffering and tears are engrained in the generic narrative and may prefigure a tragic ending, whereas the romantic comedy makes a promise to its audience that tears will be dismissed through comedy, and that adversity will be overcome. Jeffers McDonald observed that the genre developed 'an increased emphasis on the importance of tears' (2007: 85) from the late 1980s onwards, citing films such as *When Harry Met Sally* and *Sleepless In Seattle* as examples of this 'neo-traditional' cycle that share a sentimental and nostalgic tone, offering a vision of the perfect romance. The romantic comedy placed its emphasis more on romance than on comedy, as is made evident in the nostalgic tone and romantic soundtrack as the characters long for the perfect romance.

King explores how comedy is typical of popular Hollywood genres in revolving 'around the creation followed by the resolution of a specific kind of emotional tension' (2002: 8). Comedy hinges on moments of 'disruption, liberation or transgression', yet the 'disavowal of any real disturbance can occur more or less simultaneously', as the genre contract dissipates any sense of real threat for the audience. Thus, whilst we watch Susan Vance trying to capture the wild leopard, believing it to be her pet 'Baby', we know that she is not seriously in danger, as the film is a romantic comedy, as codified in the performance, soundtrack, cinematography and editing. The nature of the incongruity of the situation, the exaggerated nature of the mix-up, hinging on the narrative devices of coincidence and misunderstandings, add resonance to the comedy. Such a situation is underwritten by its sheer implausibility, which ensures that it cannot be taken seriously, fulfilling the 'logic of the absurd', which creates 'comic insulation', according to Steve Neale and Frank Krutnik (1990: 69).

The degree of implausibility must be balanced by sufficient credibility within the romantic comedy for the audience to care about what happens to the characters and to be able to relate to their feelings, situation and emotional journey. Some forms of comedy revolve around comic figures who are primarily 'clowns', with the audience remaining distanced from them, as is characteristic of the performances of the

Marx Brothers or Mr Bean, whereas the romantic comedy establishes a dominant tone 'that encourages a strong degree of emotional implication in the fate of the characters, verging on the (melo)dramatic' (King: 2002, 10). The neo-traditional romantic comedy has placed a greater emphasis on emotional engagement, as noted above, shifting the focus of the audience's response away from laughter and more towards tears and empathy. Steve Neale recognised how romantic music is used in this genre cycle in order to evoke 'the signs and values of "old-fashioned romance"' (1992: 295–96). *When Harry Met Sally* foregrounds romance in its opening frames, the soundtrack being 'It Had To Be You', instantly creating a sentimental framework for the ensuing narrative. The romantic theme is further developed by the opening scene, which features an older couple talking direct to camera about their courtship and enduring love. The documentary style adds realism and sincerity, before the film cuts to the first meeting between Harry and Sally. Comedy is created through Harry's protracted farewell to his girlfriend, observed chiefly via Sally's reaction shots, introducing the conflict that dominates their first meeting. Harry's uncouthness is contrasted with Sally's prissiness; she endeavours to explain her complex driving schedule to his backside as he delves clumsily in the back of the car, and then proceeds to spit out grape pips onto the closed window. Their journey is punctuated by verbal and visual comedy, which is underscored by the romantic tone and sense of narrative direction established in the opening titles and scene. The spectator has enough information, from knowledge of the genre as a whole, the stars, the tone of the opening sequence and the very title, to know that Harry and Sally are meant to be together. The film's romantic tone remains predominant, reinforced through continued use of romantic soundtrack and the documentary-style interviews with elderly couples that punctuate the narrative, all on the theme of love and marriage.

King cites the work of Raymond Durgnat in explaining how comedy works by balancing the detachment of the spectator with a sense of implication in that 'we are often half-aware that we have traits in common with the fictional characters on the screen'(2002: 10). The audience

Figure 4.1 Sally is appalled by Harry on their first encounter in *When Harry Met Sally*.

laugh with relief that it is not us on the screen, even to the point of feeling superior to the characters in all their foolishness and humiliation, yet we can laugh with a sense of recognition, or in sympathy with the character with whom we have been aligned. Harry is ridiculous in his oafish and insensitive behaviour; Sally is ridiculous for her desire to control and suppress her irritation with Harry, yet their characteristics are exaggerated and recognisable versions of many couples' conflicting personalities. Romantic comedy features characters who tend to be more complex and credible than in other types of comedy, as Jenkins and Karnick acknowledge: ' ... the narratives of romantic comedies are marked by the comic exaggeration of realist traits ... yet retain rounded and plausible characters ... often defined through their comic flaws' (1995: 163). Bridget Jones (Renee Zellweger) is hampered by her low self-esteem and her impetuousness, Brad (Rock Hudson) is an inveterate womaniser in *Pillow Talk*, and Ellie (Claudette Colbert) is spoilt and headstrong in *It Happened One Night*. The comic flaw leads to conflict and a difficult process of self-discovery for the characters; the audience remain distanced by the comedy yet emotionally engaged by the romance.

King comments on how comedies often deal with the failure of the individual to fit in with the institutions that dominate society, how comedy narratives 'pitch ... the central performer against unsympathetic formal institutions' (2002: 40), the individual being either a rebel or an incompetent misfit. The romantic comedy hinges on the importance of the institution of marriage, typically centring on the individual's desire for marriage or, conversely, the desire not to be married, being actively resistant to the institution. In *When Harry Met Sally*, the eponymous characters both yearn to be happily settled in an enduring partnership, struggling through a series of failed relationships. *27 Dresses* pairs Jane (Katherine Heigl), who yearns to be a bride rather than a bridesmaid, with Kevin, who is anti-marriage in the wake of his divorce. The comedies of remarriage such as *Adam's Rib* and *The Awful Truth* see the couple as failing in their marriage, rebelling against the institution, but coming ultimately to realise that they need each other, gaining a renewed faith in their marriage. Marriage is a means of restoring order and granting happiness to the characters, integrating them into society and resolving disruption and conflict. The romantic comedy is arguably more conservative than other comedies, as it respects society's structures and dominant ideologies, offering a resolution that reinforces tradition and conformity.

SUBVERSION OF THE ADULT WORLD

The screwball comedy is rather more subversive in its attitude to relationships than many later romantic comedies. Although the couple ultimately end up together, there is a repeated theme of the need to innovate marriage to order to accommodate the desire for play and rebelliousness that has characterised the couple's courtship and conflicts. The institution has to bend to accommodate the comic energies of the central characters. This was central to the Grant and Hepburn films *Holiday* and *Bringing Up Baby*, which both contrast the possible joylessness of conventional marriage with a more liberated, playful alternative. The Hepburn character represents the potential to rebel against tradition, offering a marriage that celebrates play and exuberance, offering an escape from adult responsibilities and the possibility of eternal childhood together. The comedy hinges on the rejection of the adult world and its attendant undesirable qualities that threaten the happiness of the protagonists. In *Holiday*, Johnny (Grant) and Linda (Hepburn) are at ease in the playroom of the house, where Johnny demonstrates his acrobatic prowess and Linda can be herself, as she can't be in the 'grown up' rooms lower down the house.

Comedy is about the excess of childish energies that can no longer be contained by the adult frameworks, whether they be the institution of marriage or the self-control that is expected of the individual within society. Characters say and do things that are not acceptable, they give vent to feelings that normally remain repressed. In this respect they are a threat to the stability of society, as they represent the unleashing of energies that are normally contained. Thus Johnny is prone to performing somersaults in public places; Susan Vance (*Bringing Up Baby*) has a pet leopard and performs tricks throwing olives into her mouth in the restaurant; Sally (Meg Ryan) noisily simulates an orgasm in a crowded café in *When Harry Met Sally*; and in *The Break-Up*, Gary (Vince Vaughan) and Brooke (Jennifer Anniston) wage a war of attrition on each other as each seeks to oust the other from the apartment in the wake of their separation. They try to outdo each other through a series of childish manoeuvres, including installing a pool table in the apartment, inviting dates round and hosting a strip-poker party. As Neale and Krutnik point out with reference to Freudian theory on humour, 'the infantile image ... is central to the comic', entailing powerlessness and 'the lack of co-ordination and control' (1990: 78). *The Break-Up* illustrates how the unleashed emotions that dominate the romantic comedy can result in this loss of control and power, resulting in behaviour that is comic in being infantile. On the other hand, a character may exhibit childish behaviour traits which may represent playfulness, and hence suitability to be a playmate, as with Susan Vance and Johnny. The audience may take pleasure in this comedy, as it channels our (repressed) desire to escape from the restrictions of the adult world, a vicarious enjoyment of the pleasures of release and recognition of childlike urges. Yet such childishness may signal the need to mature and take responsibility, creating conflict with other characters, as in *The Break-Up*, where the behaviour is comic in being excessive and disruptive, but simultaneously creates pathos as the couple battle over the disputed territory.

COMIC SURPRISE AND SUSPENSE

Jenkins and Karnick (1995: 80) observed that romantic comedy is based around a fundamental paradox in that it offers a tightly structured formulaic narrative which harnesses the unexpected in terms of the nature of comedy. Comedy is essentially about surprises and the unpredictable, departures from what is normal; 'the incongruous nature of humour arises from unexpected shifts away from narrative logic and continuity'. The unexpected gives delight to the spectator, in contrast to the pleasure created by following the predictable narrative path of the genre, applying Barthes's distinction between *jouissance* and *plaisir*. *Jouissance* (delight) is an uncontrolled pleasure which is difficult to rationalise, creating a more intense relationship between the film and the spectator. Comedy hinges on these moments of affective intensity, when the spectator's delight in the unforeseen involves a physical reaction. In this respect, comedy can be considered one of the more affective genres, much like horror, in terms of eliciting an affective response, manifested in a more intense relationship between text and spectator. Ellie hurling herself off her father's yacht in *It Happened One Night* and Bridget Jones turning up as a Playboy bunny at a sedate country party are both examples of how the unexpected creates comedy in the genre.

Neale and Krutnik point out the importance of distribution of narrative knowledge between the characters and the spectator in order to create comic suspense and surprise (1990: 34). There are several ways in which this narrative device can work within the romantic comedy, and it is often used in narrative frameworks, for example through the use of misunderstandings and ignorance which result in disruption. One typical use of comic suspense is when a character is involved in a scheme of which the other characters are not aware. *The Lady Eve* is used by Neale to illustrate this device, as Jean Harrington (Barbara Stanwyck) is a con artist who sets out to trap the guileless Hopsy (Henry Fonda) by making him fall in love with her. Complication ensues when she falls in love with him and decides to confess all to him, with disastrous consequences. *How To Lose A Guy In 10 Days* sets up a narrative premise which is based on each central character having a scheme to manipulate the emotions of the other, both Andie (Kate Hudson) and Ben (Matthew McConaughey) setting out to make the other fall in love with them in order to further their career. The spectator is put in a privileged position, being aware of the true intentions of each character, and thus being able to appreciate the comic ironies created through their situations. The characters each believe themselves to be in control of the situation, whilst the spectator can enjoy the irony of their delusion, understanding why they lose control as they genuinely fall in love with each other, and predicting the moment when they will learn of their mutual scheming. Comic suspense, as Neale and Krutnik point out, builds towards the moment when all is revealed to the character(s), when knowledge is gained, that is, 'anagnorisis, a transition from ignorance to knowledge' (1990: 33). The romantic comedy traces the characters' journey from unhappiness and lack of fulfilment to the resolution in which they have reached emotional maturity, self-knowledge and happiness and are united with the significant other. The spectator watches in suspense as to how they will gain this knowledge, yet can appreciate the humour created by the differing levels of knowledge amongst the characters, knowing that all will be resolved.

Disguise is another comic device that relies on these differing levels of knowledge, creating suspense as the spectator enjoys the consequences of the misunderstandings and havoc that ensue but knows that the character risks exposure and even humiliation. In *How To Lose A Guy*, Andie and Ben disguise their true personalities as part of their plot each to deceive the other; in *Pillow Talk*, Brad (Rock Hudson) transforms himself into the old-fashioned Texan, 'Rex', in order to seduce Jan

(Doris Day); and in *The Awful Truth*, Lucy (Irene Dunne) passes herself off as Jerry's (Cary Grant) drunken, vulgar sister in order to ruin his chances with the prim socialite Barbara Vance. The comedy created through disguise was often compounded by playing with gender identities, signalling further departures from normality and a sense of disruption. In *Pillow Talk*, Brad suggests that his alter ego, Rex, is gay, in order to reassure Jan and thus get even closer to her; and in *I Was A Male War Bride*, Cary Grant dresses up as a woman in order to convince the US armed forces that he is a war bride and gain entry to the States with his new wife.

THE GAG

Comic surprise can generate much of the laughter of a romantic comedy, in the guise of the unexpected event. Neale and Krutnik observe that the event may not 'follow any pre-established system of logic' and that often the 'event bears no relationship whatsoever either to the plot or to causal motivation' (1990: 42), as when David Huxley rips the back of Susan's dress by accident in *Bringing Up Baby* or when Harry spits the grape pips at a closed window in Sally's car in *When Harry Met Sally*. The sheer implausibility of these moments, compounded by the unexpectedness, accentuates the comic effect. These two comic moments are examples of the gag, which is one of the central tools used by comedy in creating laughter. The gag operates around such moments of comic surprise, when the narrative can be punctuated by moments of visual comedy. The gag may actually enhance the spectator's knowledge of a specific character, or serve to test them in order to demonstrate their weakness in the face of adversity. David Huxley is again proved to be a social incompetent upon whom the presence of Susan has a distinctly destabilising effect, resulting in actually exposing her to the general public. Harry is shown to be a man of few manners and little self-awareness, creating tension with Sally, which again is a vital stage in the chemistry that ultimately brings the romantic comedy couple together. Jenkins and Karnick (1995: 84–85) make the point that 'gags are focal points of our cognitive and affective experience of comic films', in that they demand attention and involve spectator participation in terms of affective response, and thus are highly memorable.

The gag does not have the central importance in generating laughter in the romantic comedy that it has in other comedic forms. The romantic comedy tends to rely more on narrative situation to create comedy. The gag serves to crystallise narrative themes and issues, and can have plot consequences. In *Bringing Up Baby*, David is forced to defend Susan's honour and conceal her backside from the public, taking control of the situation by holding her closely in front of him and quick-stepping her out of the restaurant, much to everyone's amusement. The two are brought even closer together as a result of this extended gag, and start to collude to defend each other from the various adversities that threaten them. David has demonstrated manly qualities in his sense of honour and his ability to take action in response to Susan's exposure, inadvertently gaining a certain intimacy with her. In return, Susan insists on sewing David's coat tails, which she had accidentally torn, resulting in his being further embroiled in her world as she offers to exploit her connections to help him gain vital funding for the museum where he works.

The gag in this case forms part of the escalating or snowballing comedy that is typical of the screwball comedy. The world of the film is beset by a madness that has been unleashed as a result of the colliding personalities of the central couple. The madness manifests itself in the extraordinary train of events that sweeps the couple from normality to a new reality, where anything is possible – Northrop Frye's 'utopian dimension' – and order can only be imposed when the two lovers are united. Neale and Krutnik examined how such gags and comic moments can be understood in the light of Freud's work *Jokes and Their Relation to the Unconscious*, in that they can be seen to 'articulate aggressive or erotic wishes … the generation of the wish takes place across the span of the narrative as a whole. The gag itself is the point at which it merely receives comic … expression' (1990: 73–74). Susan and David's accidental tearing of each other's clothes clearly articulates an erotic desire in *Bringing Up Baby*, which David seeks to repress and Susan actually recognises to some extent after talking to the psychiatrist Dr Fritz Lehman, who advises her that 'the love impulse in man frequently reveals itself in terms of conflict'.

PERFORMANCE

One important distinguishing characteristic of the romantic comedy as compared to other comedies is that it relies more on narrative situation than on performance and gags (King, 2002: 51). Nevertheless, performance is still an important source for humour. In bridging the genres of comedy and romantic melodrama, it requires greater realism in the central characters than is typical of the wider comedy genre. The romantic comedy seeks to involve the spectator in the characters' emotional journey; we need to care about their ordeals, and to applaud the inevitable ending of the couple's being united. In this respect it is important that the spectator can relate to and feel empathy for the characters. Jenkins and Karnick (1995: 154) located the romantic comedy as belonging to the tradition of 'true comedy', that is, comedy that grew out of theatrical farce, relying on plausible characters, within realistic situations, who subjugate their performance style to the demands of the narrative. This was as opposed to comedian comedy, with its background in the vaudeville tradition, where the narrative is centred on a comedian performer, notable examples being Jerry Lewis, Bob Hope and Steve Martin. Here the emphasis is on performance virtuosity and on characters who tend to be less realistic, bordering on stereotypes. Jenkins and Karnick commented how romantic comedy stars such as Katharine Hepburn and Cary Grant tended to take roles in both comedy and more dramatic films, and thus their performance can be seen to 'maintain the realism and character integration expected elsewhere within the classical cinema' (1995: 155).

The romantic comedy allows moments where performance becomes vital in creating comedy, although clearly pertaining to the narrative development. Characters may 'adopt alternative identities, lie, exaggerate, impersonate or masquerade', according to Jenkins and Karnick (1995: 151), creating a layered performance where realism is balanced with performance for its own sake, where the nature of the performance creates pleasure for the spectator and does demonstrate the star's virtuosity. In How To Lose A Guy In 10 Days, Andie maintains a performance as the clingy, whining girlfriend in order to 'lose' Ben, leading to virtuoso performances as when Ben brings his mates back to play poker. Andie railroads the evening with her dainty yet inedible snacks, coughing loudly to stop the players smoking, spoiling the game by divulging one player's hand, playing peekaboo in the kitchen hatch, blowing Ben's nose for him (whilst calling him 'Mr Sniffles'), throwing a tantrum over the symbolism of the death of their 'lovefern', and then finally throwing a plate of snacks over the players before walking out. This performance is typical of comedy in being excessive, and in being a spectacle in its own right, disrupting the diegesis. Yet, unlike much comedy, the performance is clearly within the realms of the narrative causality of the film and is typical of the nature of the layered performance that can be found in romantic comedy.

CASE STUDY: *ANNIE HALL*

Woody Allen's 1977 romantic comedy *Annie Hall* incorporates many of the comic devices that are typical of the romantic comedy. This case study will demonstrate how Allen plays with the genre's conventions, incorporating his background as a comedian to reinvigorate the romcom so as to reflect the disaffection of the 1970s in the wake of the era of sexual liberation and the second wave of feminism.

Annie Hall was a significant departure for Allen, moving away from the pure comedy of earlier films, such as *Sleeper* and *Love and Death*, to the romantic comedy. He confessed to Stig Bjorkman (2004: 75) that he had decided 'to abandon … just clowning around and the safety of complete broad comedy' in order to 'try and make some deeper film and not be as funny in the same way'. Woody Allen was an established comedian, director and actor who had found considerable success in writing for other comedians before directing his own film comedies. *Annie Hall* was his first romantic comedy, and he went on to experiment with the genre in films such as *Manhattan* and *Hannah And Her Sisters*. *Annie Hall* is frequently cited as having a considerable influence on the romantic comedy, yet paradoxically it departs significantly from the genre blueprint, as the audience are made aware from the very start of the film that the couple do not end up together; Allen himself labelled it 'a nervous comedy', indicating its tone and theme. As Frank Krutnik notes, the film 'fractures the classical ordering of romantic comedy narrative' (1998: 20) manifesting a weariness and pessimism about relationships that was very much of its era. Krutnik describes the film's 'flamboyant narrative derangement' as making 'the breakdown of structures a principal issue in the film's representation of intimate affairs', suggesting 'the difficulty of sustaining attachments in a ... world in which traditional conceptions of heterosexual intimacy have lost their authority' (1998: 20). *Annie Hall* is very pessimistic about relationships, as Woody Allen's character, Alvy, concludes in the final voiceover: ' ... they're totally irrational and crazy and absurd, but we keep going through it ... '. The characters strive to have meaningful and enduring relationships, yet not one relationship is shown to be successful, each one being a crisis that the participants are unable to control. *Annie Hall* polarises the genre, combining an uncharacteristically dark view of love and relationships with a more pronounced and self-reflexive comic mode than is typical of the romantic comedy. Allen's background as a comedian takes the genre to a new sphere of humour, embracing stand-up comedy and foregrounding the gag, serving to emphasise the dysfunctional, miserable reality of Alvy and Annie's relationship.

The film tells the story of the doomed relationship between Annie Hall (Diane Keaton) and Alvy Singer (Woody Allen). Alvy is a successful comedian, twice divorced, and a typical Allen character in being neurotic, cerebral and entirely fixed in his New York environment. Annie comes from a Wasp background, in contrast to Alvy's working-class

Jewish roots in Brooklyn. Annie is rather ditzy, yet ready to embrace life's opportunities as she pursues her creative urges as a photographer and, more successfully, as a singer. The narrative pieces together the trajectory of their relationship and its impact on the couple, particularly on Alvy, telling the story from his point of view. The couple realise that they have fundamental differences and decide on an amicable split, and Annie moves to California in order to further her singing career, living with a successful record company executive. Alvy realises that he wants Annie back but fails to win her over, and the film finishes with the couple meeting again with different partners, and being on friendly terms, as Alvy muses on the impossibility of maintaining successful relationships.

Comedian comedy and performance

Annie Hall is essentially a romantic comedy which draws heavily on the conventions of 'comedian comedy', that is, film comedy that is centred on the performance of a comedy star, the appeal of which is based on their star persona. *Annie Hall* is also a 'Woody Allen film', and as such can be judged to manifest his signature style, working within the comedy genre. The audience will be familiar with his style as a performer, as well as director, and the film's central character, Alvy, is an extension of his comic persona: the small, intense and neurotic Jewish New Yorker who is obsessed with sex, death, psychoanalysis and race. Geoff King points out that the integration of the familiar comic persona into the narrative is an extension of how stardom works in film: 'The difference in comedian comedy is generally one of degree, the comedian … being permitted greater scope to move towards the domain of outright performativity' (2002: 36).

The film discards the conventional narrative style of the romantic comedy in its opening frames as Alvy talks directly to camera, breaking the fourth wall. He strings together a series of gags, in the style of a comedian's stand-up routine, interspersing them with poignant glimpses of his despair and low self-esteem, interweaving the deeply personal with the ridiculous, the incongruity of which is central to Alvy's character, and to Allen's persona. There is a dark, ironic vein to Allen's comedy, as he is straight faced, dealing with serious themes, totally isolated within the frame, enhancing the poignancy of his sense of loss. His gag becomes a quirky way of introducing his theme, engaging the audience's laughter and, effectively, their support, before abruptly presenting his dilemma: 'Annie and I broke up and I still can't get my mind around that, you know I keep sifting the pieces of the relationship through my mind and examining my life and trying to figure out where did the screw-up come, y'know? A year ago we were in love … '. The confessional nature of his monologue bridges the affective gap between comedian and audience, created by the departure from the formulaic nature of the romantic comedy, and the audience's familiarity with Allen's persona. There is a strong autobiographical element to the narrative, lending a greater degree of emotional veracity to Alvy's plight; Woody Allen had been in a relationship with Diane Keaton, and their characters in the film have been interpreted as being based on the two of them, even though Allen has denied this.

The film foregrounds comedic performance, as is typical of 'comedian comedy' rather than romantic comedy. The narrative is suspended at points in order to allow Allen to perform in his signature style; thus we have scenes in which he actually performs as a stand-up comedian (Alvy's profession), or scenes such as Alvy's parking fiasco, which involves more physical slapstick comedy. These moments of comic virtuosity serve to disrupt the narrative and create a degree of comic insulation, distancing the audience from the characters and providing reassurance that it is not to be taken seriously. Nevertheless, the comedy also adds to the audience's implication with Alvy's predicament by reinforcing his vulnerability and haplessness. The central character of comedian comedy is typically an underdog who triumphs in the end, overcoming adversity and prevailing on his own terms, the happy ending being a defining feature of all comedy. Yet Allen's comic persona prevails in *Annie Hall*, his defining feature being failure and depressive tendencies, and Alvy finishes the film without Annie, dwelling on the impossibility of sustaining meaningful relationships.

Subversion of the adult world

The opening scene foregrounds Alvy's lack of control over his life, displaying a bemusement and helplessness which is typical of comedian-based comedy, where the central character is out of kilter with society to some extent, often being an outsider or a rebel. Alvy is an outsider, bemoaning the slightest hint of anti-Semitism, being ill at ease in any social gathering, and even becoming ill when he travels out of New York to spend time in California. Alvy is even ill at ease with himself, commenting 'I would never want to belong to any club that would have someone like me for a member. That is the key joke throughout my adult life in terms of my relationships with women.' King has observed how the comedian is often in opposition to restrictive social or collective institutions (2002: 40), and how this is often reflected in the performer's not fitting into the 'orderly institution of classical film narrative'. Alvy's inability to fit in and comply with what is expected of him results in his being arrested after a confrontation with a traffic cop who deals with the chaos created by Alvy's bumper-car approach to manoeuvring his car. Faced with the cop, Alvy becomes a nervous wreck, dropping his driving licence and then ripping it into pieces whilst explaining, 'I have a terrific problem with authority. It's not your fault ... Don't take it personal.'

The film does feature scenes of physical comedy in which the couple 'play' together, the slapstick comedy being typical of the romantic comedy in allowing the couple to experience the happiness and fulfilment of escaping the adult world together and finding each other a source of release and exhilarating energy. One such scene is when Alvy and Annie try to capture the lobsters that are rampaging around their kitchen. Alvy is terrified of the lobsters and grabs a wooden pole in order to deal with them, creating chaos in the kitchen. Annie's response is to laugh whilst getting Alvy to pose for a photo with one of the lobsters. Such moments within the romantic comedy typically signify the possibility of the couple's ability to form a relationship that integrates their childish energies and capacity for fun. Yet Alvy is unable to maintain the balance between adult and child, as he persistently takes the role of a controlling adult treating Annie as a child, voicing disapproval of her actions and tastes and endeavouring to educate her. At times of stress Alvy retreats into a pre-Oedipal state, demonstrating a childlike propensity for chaos and rebellion in the scene where he confronts the cop in Los Angeles, as is made clear in the intercutting to the bumper-car scene from his childhood. Throughout the film Allen exploits Freudian theory in gags that make reference to the impact of Alvy's childhood on his adult identity. Early in the film a flashback shows the young Alvy being told off for kissing a girl in his class. The scene departs from verisimilitude as, incongruously, the older Alvy sits at a desk and argues with the teacher in defence of the young Alvy:

ALVY: I was just expressing a healthy sexual curiosity.

TEACHER: Six year old boys do not have girls on their minds.

ALVY: I did.

GIRL: For god's sake Alvy, even Freud speaks of a latency period!

Figure 4.2 Incongruity in *Annie Hall* as the adult Alvy tries to defend his younger self.

Various children then stand up and inform us what they went on to accomplish as adults, juxtaposing their childlike demeanours with a range of increasingly unsavoury lifestyles, including heroin addiction and being 'into leather'. The comedy of the sequence is intensified by the unexpected in terms of the older Alvy's appearance in the scene, and the adult nature of the exchange. This sequence is one of many digressions from the narrative that is typical of comedian comedy, yet actually serves to develop a sense of Alvy's character and themes such as sex and adult identity. The sequence is transgressive in its representation of childhood and its stylistic devices, pushing the boundaries of what is expected and acceptable, and being typical of the film as a whole in taking the narrative into a darker comic sphere than is typical of romantic comedy.

Disruption through film language

Allen tailors the narrative formula of the romantic comedy to suit his comic persona, departing significantly from the conventional structure to incorporate his style of comedy, and incorporating signature devices such as stylistic homages to French New Wave cinema and the work of Ingmar Bergman. Allen directly addresses the audience periodically throughout the film, and uses cinematic devices such as a split screen, intercutting, subtitles and superimposition to break the rules, to disrupt the continuity and always to create laughter. In the scene with the traffic cop, Allen intercuts Alvy's driving into the other cars in the car park with images of him as a child, slamming into the other bumper cars on his father's fairground ride on Coney Island, merging past and present, and emphasising the comedy of Alvy's appalling and aggressive driving. When Alvy goes for lunch at Annie's parents' house, the camera cuts from the glaring Jew-hating grandmother to a close-up of Alvy dressed as a Hasidic Jew, disrupting the realism to create comedy through exaggeration, as the audience sees Alvy from the grandmother's point of view. Alvy then addresses the audience directly whilst the family continue eating, comparing them with his own family, leading into a split screen sequence where the two families are juxtaposed at lunch. Alvy's family's ethnic identity is comically exaggerated, in contrast to the wholesome conservatism of Annie's family. The Singers are noisy, crammed together into the shot, eating greedily, not stopping to take a breath whilst gossiping about various tragic cases of ill-health, crowded in a rather gloomy room, in contrast to the light airiness of the Halls' dining room, with the polite conversation and sophisticated table manners of a sedate middle-class household. The comedy is further enhanced by the unexpected when Mrs Hall starts to make polite conversation with Mrs Singer and the families talk between the juxtaposed shots. Allen consistently fractures the narrative unity of the film through such stylistic aberrations, which disrupt the conventional style of the romantic comedy, exuding the rebellious energy that is typical of the comedian performer.

Subverting the romantic comic conventions

Alvy and Annie are an incongruous couple in terms of their personalities, cultural and social backgrounds, and even physically. Annie is tall and elegant, with her own distinctive style of dress, in comparison to Alvy's slight frame and hesitant demeanour, his clothes and glasses suggesting him to be something of an intellectual. As their relationship develops Allen subverts the romantic comedy narrative, in yoking romance with Alvy's pessimism and neuroses. Alvy schools Annie in his particular areas of interest, taking her to see serious films such as *The Sorrow And The Pity*, and buying her books on death to read instead of the 'cat book' she is interested in, explaining 'I'm obsessed with death I think, a big subject with me. I've a very pessimistic view of life. You should know this about me if we are to go out. I feel that life is divided into the horrible and the miserable … '. Alvy's neurotic and egocentric intensity is his comic flaw, lying at the heart of Allen's comic persona and being largely to blame for his failures in relationships. Unlike the central characters of most romantic comedies, Alvy is unable to learn and to change, he cannot be redeemed by a relationship with a woman.

Ironically, Annie does learn and change in the course of their relationship, blossoming as a result of the tutelage and therapy that Alvy funded in the hope of 'improving' her mind. A split screen is used to juxtapose each of the couple with their therapists, making the comic irony of their situation clear:

ANNIE (TO HER THERAPIST): ... the thing is, since our discussions here I feel that I have a right to my own feelings. I think you would have been happy because I really asserted myself.

ALVY (TO HIS THERAPIST): The incredible thing about it is that I paid for her analysis and she's making progress, and I'm getting screwed.

The film subverts the conventions of the romantic comedy for an audience who are familiar with such narratives, creating pleasure and comedy in departing from the expected. Some of the scenes are entirely typical of the genre: the meet-cute, the montage of images of the growing romance, the misunderstandings and eventual break-up of the couple; yet the normal trajectory to reunion is blocked by departure from the fantasy of true love, to a more realistic, downbeat conclusion, where feelings are complex and love is not always requited. The 'nervous' nature of their relationship is implied through the reflexive nature of the film, showing an awareness of the genre's conventions, as when Alvy reveals his anxiety about their first kiss:

... give me a kiss ... Yes, why not? Because we're just gonna go home, later, right, and ... and ... there's just gonna be all that tension – you know, we've never kissed before, and I'll never know when to make the right move, or anything. So we'll kiss now, we'll get it over with, and then we'll go eat – ok? We'll digest our food better.

Allen mines the dynamics of a relationship in more frank detail than is typical of the genre, particularly as regards sex, which is central to the problems between Annie and Alvy. Alvy's failures in the bedroom become the subject of the humour, as in the scene when he tries to convince Annie to have sex without smoking a joint first. He tries to create an erotic ambience using a red light bulb, but Annie remains detached to the extent that we see a double image of her as her spirit sits by the side of the bed whilst her body is having sex with Alvy. Here laughter is generated in mixing the implausible with the plausible; the faltering sex life of the couple is an entirely plausible situation, yet Allen creates comedy through the visual humour of the gag of Annie sitting, bored, by the bedside whilst her body goes through the motions with Alvy.

Annie Hall is exceptional in terms of being a romantic comedy that is clearly the work of an auteur, bearing all the hallmarks of Allen's work. It is also a film that bears witness to its era in terms of its 'nervousness' in its representation of romance and relationships, and its overall pessimism, subverting fundamental conventions of the genre. Much of the comedy of the film is more typical of the comedian comedy, and in this respect the film again takes the romantic comedy into fresh territory, yet can still be seen to demonstrate more conventional comic devices. Annie Hall does not appear to target a mass audience, with its jokes making reference to arcane theory and theorists, literature, films and culture, but seems to speak more to an educated, middle-class audience. In this respect it does not offer the straightforward fantasy of romance and happy endings that is readily found in a typical romantic comedy, but questions the genre's tenets, rejecting its optimism and simplicity in favour of pessimism and complexity.

5

THE BRITISH ROMANTIC COMEDY

The decade from the mid-1990s to the mid-2000s saw a sustained period of success for British cinema, marked by the release of a series of romantic comedies. These films shared certain defining features which proved a winning formula for global success: the production company Working Title, the writer Richard Curtis and the actor Hugh Grant. Prior to this period, British cinema had not been associated with the romantic comedy genre in any significant way. There had been isolated examples of romcoms, yet not the same sustained genre cycles that characterised Hollywood output. *Four Weddings and A Funeral's* international box office success in 1994 was the beginning of the decade of the British romcom, being followed by the success of *Notting Hill*, *Bridget Jones*, *About A Boy* and *Love Actually*. *Wimbledon* in 2004 proved to be one Working Title romcom too many, receiving a critical panning and being a box office disappointment. Tim Bevan, the co-founder of Working Title, announced that ' … it's safe to say there is a certain sort of romantic comedy that we would be stupid to go out and make again. You have to evolve' (Solomons and Smith, 2004), signalling the exhaustion of the production company's take on the romcom formula.

The Working Title romcom follows a very conventional format, making it a very marketable commodity as a genre film, both at home and on a global basis. Indeed, the adherence to genre conventions has been cited as one of the reasons for its success, making it easy to attract funding, and to market and to distribute it. Annabelle Honness Roe defines this genre cycle as centring 'on the coupling of a bumbling, ineffectual British man with a beautiful, successful American woman within the upper middle-class milieu of an idealised, idyllic Britain and it features quick verbal humour often derived from transgressing particularly British social conventions' (2009: 82). Honness Roe is referring here to Four Weddings, Notting Hill and Wimbledon, yet the definition can be stretched and adapted to incorporate the other Working Title romcoms, which employ the same settings, representations and humour, with different central pairings. Bridget Jones, in the eponymous films, plays the Hugh Grant role as the ineffectual yet sympathetic central character with a disastrous love life who is rewarded for her innate goodness with a responsible, sensitive and desirable partner.

Working Title has become the most successful and enduring British film production company, having made a name for itself in producing films that seek to appeal to a transatlantic market, in contrast to its very parochial early output. Setting up in 1984, its breakthrough film was My Beautiful Laundrette (1985), the first of many collaborations with Channel 4. The film was typical of the early output of Working Title, in being a low-budget (£650 000) film, that used realistic British settings and featured characters that were very much on the margins of British society. The film was distinctively British in its style and narrative, addressing difficult contemporary themes, such as racism and sexuality. The company changed gear in the early 1990s, when it became part of Polygram, which subsequently was taken over by Universal, and thus became part of a Hollywood studio. Working Title now had access to all the resources and support that such a major player could offer, and there was a subsequent shift in the nature of its output. The films tended to target an international audience rather than a distinctively British one, as can be seen from the casting decisions, with major Hollywood stars broadening the potential target audience: Andie MacDowell in Four Weddings, Julia Roberts in Notting Hill, Renee Zellweger in the Bridget Jones movies.

Four Weddings And A Funeral was made on a relatively modest budget of £2.9 million, most of the funding being courtesy of Polygram as part of its ambition to develop a European film studio to compete with Hollywood. The film went on to become a huge hit, grossing in excess of £120 million globally, with Polygram having invested heavily in publicising the film in the USA. The film was actually released in the USA before it reached Britain, having met with a favourable reception at the Sundance Film Festival. The screenplay was written by Richard Curtis, whose name is now synonymous with the Working Title romcoms, as he went on to be involved as a writer on Notting Hill and the Bridget Jones movies, and to write and direct Love Actually.

Curtis had first established a reputation as a comedy writer on British television, subsequently working on the British romantic comedy, The Tall Guy, an early Working Title production. In the film, an American actor embarks on an affair with a nurse, but his infidelity threatens to destroy their relationship. The film was not a success at the box office, but featured certain tropes which would become the trademark of Curtis's subsequent films. The protagonist Dexter (Jeff Goldblum) is a forlorn, hopeless inadequate with a disastrous love life; one of the central couple is an American; the film is set in London; the protagonist is smitten at the first sight of his unlikely paramour Kate (Emma Thompson); and the narrative concludes with reconciliation. Much of the comedy rests on farce, with the frequent use of eccentric obscenities. Goldblum shares his flat with a quirky, yet ultimately wise, flatmate, in this case a nymphomaniac landlady.

Curtis's social and cultural milieux play an important role in creating the representations of Britain that distinguish his work. His films have often been derided by critics for sentimentalising and misrepresenting Britain. Solomons and Smith summarise them as being simply:

> A gleaming London of sunshine or snow, of middle-class heartbreaks and happy endings, where no one gets stuck on the Tube and nothing looks dirty. Cut to a beautiful American, some hilarious oddballs and a self-deprecating hero, usually played by a stammering Hugh Grant.
>
> (2004)

Set largely in London, the films tend to feature predominantly upper middle-class characters, almost all of whom seem to know each other through an elaborate network of connections, based on public school education. The London they live in is a prosperous, sophisticated, cosy world that has seen little development since the nineteenth century, revolving around Notting Hill, a part of the city that has been cordoned off by the 'chattering classes', to become the village that William Thacker (Hugh Grant) eulogises in Notting Hill. Curtis himself is from a wealthy middle-class family; he was educated at public schools (notably being head boy at Harrow), and went to Oxford. Tim Adams (2004: 5) makes the point that Curtis spent much of his childhood abroad and that his representation of Britain channels 'his boyish longings into the manufacture of a world in which crippling awkwardness and Georgian front doors and a certain disaffected way with failure were the most powerful aphrodisiacs known to woman'. Curtis lives in Notting Hill, with his partner, Emma Freud, who is part of the influential Freud dynasty and a wider network of notable connections. It is fundamentally the model for the world of Four Weddings and Notting Hill. Curtis's films are the product of a close community of creative and social alliances, forming an ensemble that unifies his work as much on the screen as behind the scenes. This sense of community is reflected in the friendship groups that support the protagonist and that are at the heart of the Curtis narrative.

One of the key unifying elements of the Working Titles romcoms is Hugh Grant, who appeared in all of the Richard Curtis romcoms until, dramatically, and prematurely, announcing his reluctance to act ever again upon the release of Bridget Jones: The Edge Of Reason, declaring: 'Making Bridget Jones was pure purgatory. It was a miserable experience. This is the last film I will ever do … ' (Honigsbaum, 2004). Robert Murphy observes that Grant 'stands in' for Curtis in Four Weddings and Notting Hill (2000: 9), given the strongly personal representations of his social milieu. As Curtis's chosen avatar, Grant's character is essentially the same in both films: the tousled-haired, public school-educated, hapless and vulnerable little-boy lost, who struggles to make his way through the hazards and challenges of his relationship with an American woman. In both films Grant plays a hapless yet charming character whose good looks and self-deprecation help to engage the audience's sympathies, even in the case of Charles in Four Weddings, who has clearly been the cause of much heartache to his previous partners, yet is at a loss as to how to manage his life any better.

Grant comes from a similar background of privilege and affluence to Curtis; educated at illustrious public schools, followed by a degree at Oxford, the two clearly share common ground. Grant's persona came to define the Working Title romantic comedy, although he has been criticised for his mannered acting style and his apparently narrow range, the Observer's film critic, Philip Norman, pronouncing that 'He's always been the same role: the sexy, smugly diffident Englishman ... From his first appearance, in Privileged, when he was still an undergraduate, through the period movies he's done with Merchant Ivory, to the Richard Curtis pictures' (Marre, 2007).

Grant is associated with a particular representation of Britishness which has helped to sell his romantic comedies to an international audience. Part of the appeal of both Four Weddings and Notting Hill is a vision of British life which owes a debt to the heritage film (as epitomised in the work of Merchant Ivory). This is a world of imposing houses and the upper classes, a world of manners and privilege, and a sense of timeless elegance. Nick Roddick comments that Four Weddings 'exports a view of British life which is much more like the rest of the world wants it to be than it actually is – a strategy that has worked very well for Merchant-Ivory over the past decade' (1995: 15). Four Weddings is more explicit in drawing on these cultural markers, but Notting Hill is still rooted in this world, with its representation of a very privileged and select West London community. Grant's persona combines a charming and vulnerable Peter Pan-like character with the essence of the heritage film, with its representations of the mythical English gentleman. Emma Thompson identified his star qualities in casting him as the unassuming vicar in Sense and Sensibility; she was 'directly responsible for a piece of self-referential casting ... Grant is used in a way that plays on his role as Charles in *Four Weddings and a Funeral* ... and is encouraged to remind us of that amiable, charming and rather hapless man' (Church Gibson, 2000: 117).

Four Weddings made Grant into a star, who moved on to Hollywood leading roles and whose on- and off-screen personae continued to merge. In 1995 his arrest for indecent conduct with a prostitute in Los Angeles created a media storm across the Atlantic, and ultimately fed through to a new variation on his screen persona – the bad boy, as in his role as Daniel Cleaver in the *Bridget Jones* films. Oliver Marre points out that Grant himself acknowledges the parallels between his screen roles and his real life, commenting on 'his similarity to the washed up, middle-aged star of his latest outing, *Music and Lyrics*' (2007: 41). Grant's film career has centred on the romantic comedy, in both Britain and Hollywood, driven primarily by his appeal to the over-25 female audience, one of the key demographics for the genre.

Working Title has not completely forsaken the romantic comedy, having produced *Pride and Prejudice* (albeit costume drama), *Definitely Maybe* (very much set in the US) and *Wild Child* (British/American teen comedy) since 2004. Nevertheless, the mould of the British Working Title romcom has been retired for the time being. Richard Curtis has also attempted to move away from the genre, with mixed results, his comedy *The Boat That Rocked* (2009) having disappointed at the box office and received a critical drubbing.

CASE STUDY: *FOUR WEDDINGS AND A FUNERAL* (1994)

The narrative of *Four Weddings* hinges on the central couple falling in love at first sight and their struggle to establish a permanent relationship. The couple have significant differences: Charles is quiet and polite, self-effacing and, despite his obvious attraction for women, unsuccessful in love, having a series of ignominious relationships behind him. Whereas Carrie (Andie Macdowell) is a feisty, confident American, who has slept with thirty-three men and has a clear sense of purpose, in contrast to Charles's indecisive and hesitant demeanour. The couple meet at a sequence of four weddings and a funeral, each occasion marking a different stage in their courtship. The fourth wedding is that of Charles and a previous ex; Carrie turns up by herself, having separated from her husband, and consequently Charles is unable to go through with the ceremony. The film finishes with a mutual declaration of love and a photo of the couple with a baby.

The couple is more or less repeated in Notting Hill, where William (Hugh Grant) is the unassuming and lonely Englishman, who lacks confidence in relationships after the failure of his marriage. Julia Roberts is cast as the confident and beautiful Anna, a Hollywood movie star, who, like Carrie, makes the first move in initiating their relationship and has to take the leading role throughout much of the narrative. This opposition in terms of nationality is equated with personal qualities: confidence is juxtaposed with uncertainty, sexual experience with reticence, the active with the passive, the outsider with the familiar, the new with the traditional. Grant's character seems to symbolise a version of Englishness which is contrasted with the more radical destabilising elements, encapsulated in the 'other' that is both female and foreign. His inertia is challenged, and he ultimately embraces and accepts change, yet on his terms, enabling an enduring relationship to be established.

The casting of a major Hollywood star in the role of Grant's love interest is indicative of Working Title's new, more expansive agenda in the wake of its takeover by Polygram (and subsequently Universal). Four Weddings has an acute awareness of an American audience and signals a desire to move away from the perils of the British film industry, circumscribed by limited budgets and limited box office returns, just as Carrie, the American, offers Charles hope, and a future that lifts him out of his apathy. Carrie, packaged in designer clothing, charm and good manners, represents a challenge to Charles's world. Her first appearance, though, signals her difference and her suitability as a partner for Charles, when she manages to 'out-late' him at the first wedding in the narrative. She instantly becomes the centre of attention as heads turn in expectancy, cutting a glamorous figure in a hat the size of a small flying saucer, making a style statement that hints at her 'difference'. Charles, whose late arrival had not been quite as coolly executed as Carrie's, mutters 'I hate people being late, hate it', his own lateness being a leitmotif throughout the film. Charles is instantly drawn to Carrie, as a result of her lateness and her hat – upon which he compliments her.

Carrie is established as a mysterious character from the start, in common with Anna in Notting Hill, there is a pervading sense of enigma – the enigma of the female, but also of the foreign. This enigmatic quality remains as the audience are aligned with Charles, who is clearly at a loss to understand relationships, and women in general. Yet Carrie simultaneously represents an openness and a lack of inhibition that attract Charles. When he enquires as to who she is, Fiona's (Kristen Scott Thomas) answer is coloured by her unrequited love for him as she sneers: 'American ... Slut ... Used to work at Vogue, lives in America now. Only goes out with very glamorous people. Quite out of your league.' Carrie's nationality evokes mystique and sexual sophistication as the camera cuts away to a point-of-view shot showing her, dressed stylishly, yet not exposing any flesh, talking to a couple of elderly women. Fiona's attitude comes across as jealous, but also that of a snob. Fiona is represented as an upper-class beauty, yet one whose beauty is sterile and isolated, as she fails to initiate a successful relationship. Her archetypal British froideur stands in contrast to Carrie's warmth. Charles is not attracted by Fiona, signalling the need for Britain to look outwards, rather than inwards, to embrace difference and openness.

Initially, Carrie is very open about her feelings towards Charles as she initiates their first night together, masquerading as his wife in order to get him to herself and up to her room. Under the watchful eye of the Virgin Queen, Elizabeth I, whose portrait is prominent on the wall, Carrie seduces the willing Charles, their dialogue reinforcing their cultural differences:

CARRIE: I noticed the bride and groom didn't kiss in the church, which is kinda strange. Where I come from kissing is very big.

CHARLES: ... I think you're right. I think we are probably more reserved and you know, 'you may kiss the bride' isn't actually in the Book of Common Prayer.

CARRIE: I always worry I'd go too far, you know, in the heat of the moment.

CHARLES: How far do you think 'too far' would be then?

She proceeds to kiss Charles. Carrie is a male fantasy, the American girl who takes the lead in seducing the shy Brit; she is the type of girl that Colin (Kris Marshall) travels across the Atlantic to find in order to get the sex that he can't get in Britain in *Love Actually*. This liberated sexuality is represented as intriguing and liberating for both Charles and Colin in turn. Carrie's carefree demeanour is a breath of fresh air in comparison to Charles's former girlfriends, who are represented en masse at the second wedding in the narrative. Charles is forced to confront their resentment, anger and upset, creating a damning track record of relationship disasters for him. Carrie rescues him again, whisking him away to her hotel and another passionate night together. Charles remains inert and passive, letting the relationship happen, whereas Carrie *makes* things happen. Her greater experience makes Charles seem quaint and old fashioned when she reels off her impressive list of sexual liaisons. Carrie reveals that she has had thirty-three lovers, hinting at a diverse sexual history, clearly making Charles feel inadequate in comparison, as he admits to having had 'nothing like that many, I don't know what the fuck I've been doing with my time actually ... '. Rather than Carrie seeming like the 'slut' that Fiona labelled her, Charles is clearly impressed and intrigued by her.

Charles is not the only character who finds happiness with an American, as his flatmate Scarlett (Charlotte Colman) meets an imposing Texan at Carrie's wedding, who goes on to become her husband. Scarlett is characteristically outspoken, confessing that 'I always imagine that Americans are going to be dull as shit, but I mean of course you're not, are you … You're lovely.' They are an incongruous couple, the suave good looks of Chester paired with Scarlett's quirkiness, yet she too embraces American culture, pictured in a white cowboy's outfit in her wedding photo in the closing montage.

Four Weddings has been accused of packaging England for an American audience, with its upper-class settings and characters and its debt to the heritage film. Sarah Street commented on how the film 'displays a fascination with the upper classes, featuring numerous ceremonies, at which they, their clothes and possessions are on full display' (1997: 110). Fiona and Tom are brother-and-sister wealthy landowners, with servants and a vast house – 'one hundred and thirty-seven rooms, actually' – Tom being the seventh-richest man in the country. The film builds on the archetype of the eccentric upper class, as Tom is represented as lovable, but rather dim and absent minded. We first see him waking up in his stately home, where a wellington boot has been left on his bureau, and he continues to provide easy laughs with his various pratfalls throughout the film. This representation of Britain is fixated on the iconography of the world of Country Life and Tatler: the stately home, the country church, the elaborate celebrations, the Landrover, the quaint English pub, the tartan and bagpipes of tourists' Scotland. The film is punctuated by a sequence of establishing shots that dwell on idyllic landscapes: the rural idyll, the Scottish glen and the River Thames. Four Weddings offers a nostalgic image of Britain that is typical of the romantic comedy in building a fantasy that shirks realism in favour of the fairy tale. In this respect, the film respects a tradition that was established in the screwball comedies of the late 1930s and early 1940s, such as Bringing Up Baby, The Philadelphia Story and Holiday, whose characters and settings are predominantly those of the moneyed classes. Honness Roe makes reference to Andrew Higson's work on British cinema when she observes that Four Weddings' representation of British culture 'can be read as symptomatic of the time of uncertain national identity' (2009: 91) at the end of the twentieth century, as Britain becomes increasingly dependent on the USA both culturally and politically.

Charles is at a crisis point in his life at the start of the film, enduring the spectacle of endless ceremonies marking the commitment of his friends to marriage, yet unable to take that step himself. As he confesses in his best man's speech at the first wedding: 'I am as ever in bewildered awe of anyone who makes this kind of commitment that Laura and Angus have made today. I know I couldn't do it, and I think it's wonderful they can.' Charles is a dreamer, though, and believes in true love, knowing that Carrie is the one for him, yet circumstance and timing seem to be against him attaining his heart's desire. Upon learning about Carrie's engagement he is beset by self-doubt: 'What the hell's going on here? Why am I always at weddings and never actually getting married? … Maybe I have met the right girl, maybe I meet the right girls all the time. Maybe it's me.' He confides to Tom after Gareth's funeral, 'There is such a thing as a perfect match. If we can't be like Gareth and Matthew, then, maybe we should just let it go.' As Tom points out in response, Charles believes in 'the thunderbolt' of true love, fitting for the hero of a romantic comedy. Charles is at a low point after the funeral, as reflected in the dingy greyness of the industrial mise-en-scène, away from the pastoral idyll that characterises the wedding scenes. He subsequently goes against his instincts and prepares to marry Hen, his neurotic ex-girlfriend, seemingly sacrificing himself to social expectation.

Whereas most of Charles's friends yearn for commitment and traditional relationships in the form of marriage, Charles struggles with society's expectations and ultimately comes to form his own rules, which he hesitantly proposes to Carrie: 'Do you think … after we've spent some more time together, that you might agree [pause] not to marry me? And do you think not being married to me might be something you'd consider doing for the rest of your life?' Charles is liberated by the impact of Carrie, and all she represents, on his life. For once, he has taken control of his life by walking out of his wedding and recognising his emotional needs, no longer having to rely on the woman to lead. Nevertheless, it was his brother who interrupted the wedding ceremony, and Carrie made the journey to his house through

Figure 5.1 The couple surrender to nature in *Four Weddings and a Funeral*.

the rain to see him, whilst he is bereft and full of self-hatred, slumped at his kitchen table. The ending of the film is imbued with the spirit of the romance, with a rain-soaked embrace, as Geoff King observes 'a highly conventional signifier of openness to "nature" and the kind of disregard for institutionalised social restraint which is typical of the [romantic comedy]' (2002: 58).

It marks their freedom to be together and to be uninhibited in their feelings towards each other, just as they are uninhibited in forming a relationship that is theirs, rather than one circumscribed by the manners and conventions of society.

Four Weddings takes the box office appeal and successful track record of the British heritage film, its imagery of the rural idyll and upper-class privilege, and fuses them with the conventions of the romcom in order to appeal to a transatlantic audience. Working Title's romantic comedies recognise the essence of the 'special relationship' between Britain and the USA in their central coupling of the American and the Englishman, within the wider context of the close political ties between the two countries.

CASE STUDY: *WIMBLEDON* (2004)

Wimbledon helped to mark the end of this cycle of British romcoms. It repeated the formula of the charming yet hapless Brit coupled with the smart successful American woman, against a backdrop of quaint Englishness, as encapsulated in that institution of British tradition and gentility: Wimbledon. Significantly, neither Curtis nor Grant was involved (Grant was lined up for the male lead, but was deemed too old when the film was finally made), and the film was scripted by an American husband-and-wife team (Jennifer Flackett and Mark Levin). As Tim Adams points out in his review, 'Whereas the previous Curtis-esque films have been expertly packaged British offerings for the American market, this takes the process a stage further by offering an American vision of that transatlantic product. As such it is about as far removed from any England you have ever inhabited as Frasier Crane's housekeeper' (2004: 5). Both the male lead actor, Paul Bettany, and the director, Richard Loncraine, were new to the romantic comedy genre, seeming to offer the possibility of taking the Working Title blueprint in a new direction. Nevertheless, critics panned the film for merely seeming to rehash the Curtis formula as established in *Four Weddings*, *Notting Hill* and *Love Actually*.

The film centres on a British tennis star, Peter Colt (Paul Bettany), whose career is fading, yet who has an opportunity to compete as a wild card at Wimbledon. He holds little hope of succeeding and intends to retire after the tournament. He encounters feisty young American tennis star Lizzie Bradbury (Kirsten Dunst) in a meet-cute situation, when he mistakenly walks into her hotel room only to find her naked in the shower, much to his embarrassment and her amusement. The pair quickly become involved and, as a result, Peter starts to gain a new confidence on the court, winning his games. Lizzie's ambitious and controlling father (Sam Neill) tries to come between the two lovers and almost succeeds when his daughter is knocked out of the tournament. Ultimately, Peter wins Wimbledon and wins the girl.

Peter is a variation on the Grant character who dominates the Working Title romcom. He is the good guy who has lost his way in life, lacking confidence and self-esteem. In common with *Notting Hill*, *Love Actually* and *About A Boy*, the film opens with a voiceover that quickly aligns the audience with the hapless, self-deprecating hero, describing himself as 'a tired good-looking fellow' whose best years are behind him. In common with the Grant hero, Peter is at a crisis point in his life, having exhausted his options and needing to find a new direction. His voiceover informs us that he is now seeded number hundred and nineteen in the world, 'sport is cruel ... one hundred and eighteen guys out there are faster, stronger, better and younger, and it gets you thinking ... For the first time in my life I'm afraid ... of what happens if the ball keeps going by me.' The camera tracks back, fixing on his look of despair as he misses the ball at this point. He is suffering from a crisis in his sense of his virility and identity; he can no longer perform to the levels of which he was capable in the past and needs to find a new niche for himself in the world. Peter's mother, Augusta Colt (Eleanor Bron), confronts him with his hopeless situation:

AUGUSTA COLT: I hear you're planning to retire, to babysit a bunch of old ladies. It's not what your father and I had in mind … I believe you to be a truly *great* tennis player, you've just always been afraid to admit it to yourself!

PETER: I'm not afraid, I'm old … in tennis years I might as well be your age. I'm tired of hotels, I'm tired of airports and long-distance love affairs that never go anywhere …

Peter, much like the Grant characters in *Four Weddings* and *Notting Hill*, seems to be in a state of inertia, which could be read as the inertia of a country, not just an individual. He too is rescued from this state by the exuberance, confidence and energy of a woman, an American woman. Traditional gender roles are typically reversed as the woman takes the first step and quickly seduces the shy Englishman, becoming the catalyst that spurs him on to winning ways. Up until he meets Lizzie, Peter's fate seems to be as a heartthrob for the admiring 'old ladies' at the tennis club, reinforcing his fading virility. Lizzie is unfazed when Peter walks into her room and sees her naked in the shower, whereas Peter is overcome by awkwardness and embarrassment, mistaking her kitchen for the exit. She then proves herself his equal in a challenge during a practice session, egging him on to do better. Peter responds to her flirtation by offering her fish and chips and she responds by telling him, 'win this one, and I'll sleep with you'. The contrast between his archetypal British gesture and her direct proposition draws on the representations of British and American culture which are characteristic of the Working Title romcoms. Peter desires Lizzie but lacks the nerve to do anything about it, whereas the American is direct and uninhibited.

For Peter, the relationship has an instant, beneficial effect on his game, as he seems to absorb determination and grit from Lizzie. When she cheers him on in his second round, his game turns around and he starts to win. Love, and sex, seem to nurture Peter's virility and he becomes a greater player. When Lizzie leaves to return to the States, Peter starts to lose the men's singles final, yet manages finally to win after being reunited with her in the changing rooms during a break for rain. Lizzie gives him a pep talk, assures him of her love, and thus he is able to win. The irony in this situation is that it is Lizzie who is represented as the aggressive, ruthless player in the mould of John McEnroe who has a reputation for haranguing the umpire, which she admits is all part of firing herself up to win. These qualities are represented as being anathema to the British, Peter's father having brought him up to believe that tennis is a 'gentleman's game'. Lizzie despairs of the British and their 'apologising'.

Nevertheless, Lizzie is knocked out, blaming Peter for distracting her when she needed to focus. Typically of a romantic comedy, the couple both have to learn important lessons in order to be together: Peter becomes a winner, learning to have faith in his abilities, whereas Lizzie learns that winning isn't everything and has to reconcile her career with the need for love and emotional fulfilment. This is very much the lesson that Anna learns in Notting Hill, that her career and public image isn't everything, that she needs William's love to be truly happy. In the closing scene we learn that Peter has moved to the States, having realised 'that I was always afraid that my life would be over if I wasn't playing tennis, but the truth is, it was really just beginning'. Lizzie has gone on to become a tennis champion at the US Open and Wimbledon. Britain and America are shown to benefit from a symbiotic relationship, each half of the partnership benefiting from the union.

The contrasting parents also serve to reinforce the cultural differences. The Colts' home is an eccentric yet homely mansion that suggests past wealth; this is a family that has seen better days, seemingly symbolic of the country as a whole. The parents are too absorbed in their marital feud to take much notice of their children; the father has absented himself to live in an elaborate tree house, whereas the bohemian mother sits in the midst of her vegetable garden, in a scene reminiscent of Peter Rabbit. Peter's younger brother is a chain-smoking cycling enthusiast who enjoys fornicating, watching fornication on film and placing bets on his brother losing – essentially, playing the Rhys Ifans role from *Notting Hill*, as Philip French points out in his *Observer* review (2004).

Conversely, Lizzie's father is controlling, domineering and interfering, sharing his daughter's ambition and doing his best to ward off Peter in order to achieve success. His attributes build on certain characteristics which are perceived as being distinctively American, in contrast to the inertia and lack of ambition of the Colt family. Peter's mother complains that his father is in 'a stupor' and needs to be 'propelled to act'. Indirectly, Lizzie's influence brings new happiness to the family, as Peter discovers when he interrupts his parents having sex in the kitchen, having been brought together by his success. Even Peter's brother finds that his sibling's success results in an abundance of sex.

Wimbledon is a fantasy, with its fairy-tale narrative and various magical tropes that are typical of the Working Title romcom. Robert Murphy's study of the 1990s British romantic comedy described these films as 'urban fairy tales' whose narrative structure and situations owe much to the traditional fairy tale (2001: 297). The narrative will revolve around a magical quest, bringing together a modern prince and princess, taking them to some magical place away from their normal world, where they discover their true feelings for each other. England is represented as a magical domain of plenty, encompassing the genteel environs of the tennis club, the fading splendour of the Colts' family pile, the Dorchester hotel and, of course, Wimbledon. Peter's sports car speeds along empty streets, his journey taking in the quasi-Mediterranean glamour of the Brighton seafront and Buckingham Palace. Above them all, a magical comet lights up the night sky, an omen that something unusual and miraculous is going happen.

Peter and Lizzie are the prince and princess, of course, distinguished by their sports-star status and their beauty. Lizzie is the centre of attention from the start, yet her star status rubs off onto Peter as he starts to win his games, and they become a golden couple at the end.

Figure 5.2 Brighton's quasi-Mediterranean splendour as backdrop for the romance in *Wimbledon*.

Peter's magical quest is to win Wimbledon, and the hand of his princess. There is a mediaeval resonance to Peter's trysts on the tennis court as he seeks to conquer his various favoured opponents. Typically of such a magical narrative, his final showdown is with the villainous Jake Hammond (Austin Nichols), the arrogant American champion and rival for the hand of Lizzie. Peter has to humiliate Jake in order to become the ultimate British fantasy, a British Wimbledon champion, and it is notable that he has to defeat the conceited American to do this. This victory is indicative of the ambiguity inherent in the representation of the cultural differences as British sportsmanship triumphs, winning the tournament and the princess. It takes the impact of American determination and energy to enable Peter to win, yet British quirkiness and gentility are represented as preferable to the conceit and brattishness of the American. Ultimately, Peter and Lizzie's partnership harnesses the best of both sides of the Atlantic.

Wimbledon is a romantic comedy that is entirely conventional of the British cycle of the 1990s/2000s, yet it draws on the conventions of the sports film genre, and hence sets itself apart from the Curtis rom-coms. Robert Hanks describes the film as 'Notting Hill plus motivational psychology' in his 2004 review in *The Independent*. The film features extended sports sequences, parading an array of special effects to create a convincing sense of excitement and realism; the narrative focuses on the underdog who comes good, going through a trajectory of success followed by reversals, then ultimately victory and universal recognition. The film starts with Peter's voiceover talking of the power of dreams, suggesting his disillusion, but by the end of the film, he talks of how his dreams have come true, but, being a romantic comedy, winning wasn't everything, and love had led to a future that had surpassed his dreams. Love was responsible for making him, and Lizzie, into winners.

Over a ten-year period the Working Title romantic comedies form a coherent cycle which conforms tightly to the conventions of the genre, yet clearly purvey a distinctive image of Britain at the turn of the century that is idealised and escapist. Most of the films were successful at the box office, on a global basis, making a star out of Hugh Grant and helping to consolidate Working Title's position as the most successful British film production company. Working Title was successful in commandeering a Hollywood genre that had not been pursued with significant success within the British film industry and in tailoring it to appeal to an American audience.

6

THE STARS OF THE ROMANTIC COMEDY

The publicity engendered by a star's life beyond the screen continues to be a major factor in developing the star persona. It can be argued that the romantic comedy centres on stars whose personal lives become more relevant to their roles than seems to be the case in other genres. The romcom star tends to have a highly publicised personal life, the tumultuous details being widely available through the media. Perhaps this is increasingly the case in our twenty-four-hour, media-intensive culture, where celebrity news commands a high premium amongst producers and audiences. Jennifer Anniston, Jennifer Lopez and Renee Zellweger are examples of stars who have featured prominently in the gossip columns as their love lives have developed a narrative that shadows their film roles. The roles become mere commentaries on their torrid romances, as their films' narratives are, ironically, enhanced by our knowledge of the 'true' life narratives, which often seem to preclude any happy ending, giving their performances an authenticity that bridges the distance between star and audience.

It has clearly been the case that with most romantic comedy stars there is a marked intersection between the on-screen and off-screen personae. Katharine Hepburn's unconventional long-term liaison with the resolutely married Spencer Tracy is ironically refracted in their movies together, which offer a comparatively conventional image of courtship and married life that was never to be the case off the screen. The reputedly fiery nature of their relationship in real life appears to inform the lively exchanges and clashes of values and personalities that became the trademark of their films together. *Woman Of The Year* casts Hepburn as a successful career woman, Tess, who fails to be a successful wife to Sam (Spencer Tracy) as she continues to prosper in her career. Tess has to learn a difficult lesson and become more in touch with her feminine side so as to make the marriage work. The film ends with the couple reconciled, yet Tess having to concede her inadequacies as a wife to the long-suffering Sam. Off screen, a relationship was developing between Hepburn and Tracy which seemed to revolve around a similar collision of lifestyle and personality: Hepburn being the East Coast sophisticate from a distinguished wealthy family, daughter of a prominent feminist activist, whereas Tracy was from an Irish Catholic working-class background. They were to star in a total of nine films together, the majority being romantic comedies, yet neither of them would speak openly of their real-life relationship, and Tracy remained married to his wife until he died. Their romantic comedies built on their conflicting personae, often reflecting the gender tensions of the time, particularly the conflict between home and work as found in the career woman comedies of the 1940s, such as *Woman Of The Year*, *Adam's Rib* and *Pat and Mike*.

There are other notable star couples who developed conjoined star personae in their films together within the romantic comedy genre. Myrna Loy and William Powell were described as the most prolific screen couple in Hollywood's history, having made fourteen films together, including the popular *Thin Man* series during the 1930s and 1940s. Doris Day and Rock Hudson made three successful sex comedies together – *Pillow Talk*, *Lover Come Back* and *Send Me No Flowers* – between 1959 and 1964, which paired the girl-next-door appeal of Day with the pin-up, rugged good looks of Hudson. For the audience of the time, the star image of Day combined the glamour of her Hollywood profile as an established singer and actor with the apparent domestic normality of her marriage to the producer, Marty Melcher, and her role as a mother. Her partnership with Hudson conjoined her 'normality' with the playboy bachelor who is then made safe in his commitment to Day. The films provided an escapist fantasy for their audience, but have been subsequently revisited in the light of Hudson's homosexuality, which remained a secret until his death from AIDS, and Day's gay following. This knowledge of the extra-textual circumstances leads to a new sensitivity to the significance of the deceptions and masquerades that pervade the narratives of these films, and adds an ironic nuance to the playboy persona that Hudson performs in their first two films together. In *Pillow Talk* the playboy Brad (Hudson) endeavours to persuade Jan (Day) that he is a Texan oil tycoon as part of his elaborate plan to seduce her, taking the masquerade even further in suggesting he may have gay tendencies by showing particular interest in cooking and soft furnishings. Whereas in *Lover Come Back* (Jerry) Hudson gains the affections of Carol (Day) by pretending to be a shy, noble-minded inventor who has never been kissed by a woman. In both films the Hudson character conceals his voracious womanising by masquerading as a man whose sexuality is no threat to the sensible Doris Day character.

Woody Allen's nervous comedies tended to be strongly auto-biographical in nature, centring on a couple that often clearly mirrored his off-screen relationships. *Annie Hall*'s depiction of the tempestuous relationship between Alvy and Annie was based on the relationship between the two actors, Allen and Diane Keaton. Keaton's real name is Diane Hall, and her character was clearly based on Keaton, from the use of her own distinctive fashion style to the ambitions as a photographer and singer. Likewise, it is difficult to distinguish where the persona of Alvy Singer ends and that of Woody Allen begins, both being neurotic, Jewish comedians whose lives are centred in New York. The radical nature of his romantic comedies burrows deeply into the psyche of their neurotic auteur, seemingly making public the essence of the private in films such as *Annie Hall* and *Manhattan*.

For some romcom stars this convergence of the film role and off-screen persona seems to brand the star with an image which makes it difficult for them to move beyond the genre. Hugh Grant is an example of a star who has developed his persona through a string of notable romantic comedies, yet has made some effort to move outside the genre but failed to find significant success in these roles, notably in the crime capers *Mickey Blue Eyes* and *Small Time Crooks*. Grant has repeatedly made deprecating remarks about his roles and profession, implicitly manifesting a disdain for the genre which is prevalent amongst certain factions of more highbrow cultural commentators. Stars such as Meg Ryan, Jennifer Lopez and Jennifer Anniston have also tended to be circumscribed by the genre, and find it difficult to move successfully outside its confines.

The female stars of the genre certainly seem to suffer from the restricted shelf life that Hollywood imposes on their careers, the possibilities for an older female romcom star being very limited. Middle-aged female actors have struggled to find significant roles in the ageist culture that dominates the film industry and society as a whole, and this has been particularly notable as the careers of stars such as Meg Ryan have petered out as they enter early middle age. It could be argued that the patriarchal nature of Hollywood is responsible for prolonging the careers of male romcom stars, relative to their female co-stars, with actors such as Cary Grant, William Powell and, more recently, Hugh Grant taking leading roles well into their forties, often playing characters who are younger than themselves. Nevertheless, since the 1990s it seems that the female star has tended to be more significant in opening a romantic comedy than the male star, which may be of little surprise, given the gendered nature of the genre's audience. There are few notable contemporary male romcom stars, who are defined by the genre in a similar way to female stars such as Kate Hudson and Jennifer Lopez. Matthew McConaughey is one star who has developed his career within the genre and had little success in other genres; in the words of John Patterson, 'he's favoured us with some of the laziest, least charming, unfunny romantic comedies … alternating with damp-squib thrillers'.

He concludes that McConaughey's career is a critical flop (Patterson, 2009), seeming to draw on the pervasive critical disapproval of the genre, tinged by a suggestion that maybe it is not sufficiently manly for a respectable actor. McConaughey's name is not enough in itself to open a romantic comedy, having been paired with Sarah Jessica Parker (*Failure To Launch*), Kate Hudson (*How To Lose A Guy In 10 Days* and *Fool's Gold*) and Jennifer Lopez (*The Wedding Planner*).

Often the male star of the romantic comedy has tended to be associated with the wider comedy genre, hopefully appealing to a wider male audience, as seems to be the case with Ben Stiller, Owen Wilson and Adam Sandler. A distinct contemporary trend has been to centre some romantic comedies on a male perspective, rather than a female perspective, with a male comedy star actually leading the cast. This is part of a wider repositioning of the genre, as seen in the emergence of the 'hommecom' and 'bromance'. Comedians such as Simon Pegg (*Run Fat Boy Run*) and Will Smith (*Hitch*) have been used to open romantic comedies, leading the cast and helping to extend the appeal to a broader, male audience.

The male stars who most strongly define the genre have tended to be of a certain type: debonair, manly and good looking, exuding a charm and charisma that is difficult to resist. Stars such as Cary Grant, William Powell and Rock Hudson were variations of this archetype, being objects of desire for the female audience, but also having an aspirational appeal for the male audience. Yet in contrast, the female stars tend to be pretty, often in an off-beat, 'kooky' way, perhaps making them easier for the female audience to relate to. Doris Day, Meg Ryan and Renee Zellweger are examples who conform to this type, with their blonde good looks, which are not conventionally beautiful, but rather quirky in their appeal. This quirkiness is reflected in their star personae and becomes central to their film roles, all of them embodying an all-American attractiveness that is approachable and engaging. Peter William Evans, in his study of Meg Ryan, describes her as having a 'good girl' persona on screen which is exaggerated in her off-screen public image, quoting Iley ' ... And that nose – it screws itself up, rabbit twitch, rabbit twitch, hello aren't I cuter than cute, safer than safe' (Iley, 1993: 6–7, quoted in Evans, 1998: 199). As Evans goes on to point out, the star is 'a mixture of ordinary and extraordinary components held in tension in order to keep the audience at once reassured by the former and over-awed by the latter.' The female stars' looks tend to emphasise the 'ordinary' in this equation, whereas the classic romantic comedy male stars tend to emphasise the extraordinary in terms of aesthetics. The male star is a fantasy figure who becomes accessible to the female audience, as the romantic comedy serves as a space in which to exercise fantasies and mirror an enhanced reality where dreams come true and the dream man is a reality for the 'ordinary' woman.

The relationship between star and genre is symbiotic, in that the star defines the genre, yet in turn the genre defines the star. In any era a star may come to define the direction the genre may take, their star image structuring the appeal of the romantic comedy for its audience. The star persona has to conform to the conventions of the genre, yet be relevant to the wider contemporary context: Katharine Hepburn's persona was a confluence of the offbeat wit and charm of the screwball heroine with the feisty independence that needed to be reined in that reflected the gender tensions of the time. Yet, at the same time the star's persona will evolve through their roles, both within and outside the genre. As Patrick Phillips identifies, 'the star persona often evolves in relation to the requirements of a particular genre, with individual genre films providing "vehicles" for the star to do "their thing" … The star may depend on the opportunities the genre conventions provide' (Phillips, 1996: 184). Doris Day's career was revived by her move into the romantic comedy genre, after the decline in popularity of her musicals and of her appeal as a singer. Her star persona was redefined in turn, as she became a comedy actor rather than a singing star, channelling the wholesome, effervescent attractiveness of her former roles into the romantic comedy genre. Her popularity and appeal led to a peak in popularity for the sex comedies of the later 1950s and early 1960s, until her persona and the genre started to look dated with the advent of the 'swinging sixties'.

CASE STUDY: RENEE ZELLWEGER

Zellweger has been one of the foremost Hollywood stars of the 2000s, having had some of her most successful roles within the genre of romantic comedy. Her career-defining role was as the eponymous hero in the two movies *Bridget Jones's Diary* and its sequel, *Bridget Jones: The Edge of Reason*, and she went on to star in a diverse range of romantic comedies, including *Down With Love*, *Leatherheads* and *New In Town*. The very diversity of her romantic comedies is typical of the postmodern sensibility that has informed the contemporary genre cycle. As Krutnik observed the genre has taken a playful turn, acknowledging previous genre films, referencing and playing with the form and conventions of the genre. Krutnik refers to the work of Umberto Eco in observing that 'new forms of communication are required within a postmodern culture haunted by the presence of the "already said"' (Krutnik, 1998: 28). Zellweger's films pay homage to the past, whether it be in ironic references to older texts, as in *Down With Love*, or in recalling a particular cycle of the genre, as in the latter, which explicitly references *Pillow Talk*, or in the attempt to make a screwball comedy with *Leatherheads*.

Zellweger is notable for her success in bucking the trend of the romantic comedy star and moving successfully into other genres, with her roles in costume dramas such as *Cold Mountain* and *Miss Potter*, and in the musical *Chicago*. She has been most prolific within the romantic comedy genre, yet there is an implicit tension in her persona which hints at an unease with the genre and with her star image, which, in turn, has come to be defined by the genre. Zellweger has also had a very high-profile private life, in common with other romantic comedy female stars in particular, which has become central to her star persona.

Much of the media attention given to Zellweger focuses on her middle-class upbringing in Texas, her European parents and her academic background. She is constructed as an all-American girl, on the one hand, yet simultaneously offers something rather exotic and sophisticated, with her Norwegian mother, Swiss father and degree in

English. David Thomson describes how 'The furnace blast of southern Texas weather shows in Renée's face: the sagging lips, the moist skin, the blue eyes used to narrowing against the glare of the sun, and the colour of her hair that matches the blonde look of grass at the end of summer' (Thomson, 2001), evoking an image of natural American beauty, personifying the American landscape. Columnists often dwell on how Zellweger is different to the typical Hollywood starlet, and this difference has become more pronounced in her publicity as her career has progressed. 'Renee Zellweger isn't a Hollywood product. Indeed after graduating the University of Texas at Austin, she made local indie movies', enthuses Susan Braudy (2009).

Zellweger's breakout role was as Tom Cruise's love interest in *Jerry Maguire* (1996), for which she garnered critical approbation. She plays a working single mother who pledges her allegiance to her sacked boss in his decision to go it alone. Reviews focused on her down-to-earth charm and refreshing appeal, suggesting an endearing simplicity that she brings to the role. Roger Ebert enthused about her 'loveability' (Ebert, 1996), and Janet Maslin describes her 'open, eager, unconventionally pretty face [that] suggests miracles are in the offing ... This refreshing actress is an inspired choice ... Her fetching ordinariness, which happens to be quite extraordinary, brings [Maguire] down to earth in ways no movie queen can manage' (Maslin, 1996). This emphasis on the ordinary and the natural defines Zellweger's star persona at this early stage of her career, making her easily 'knowable' for the audience.

It was the qualities of 'loveability' and ordinariness that led to the casting of Zellweger in her first major leading role, as Bridget Jones. The film is an adaptation of a bestselling book, the diary of a 32-year-old single woman who is desperate to find love and commitment before it's too late, struggling with her weight and consumption of fags and booze along the way. The plot follows her path to true love as she becomes embroiled in a disastrous affair with the arch-cad Daniel Cleaver (Hugh Grant), going on to find Mr Right in the shape of the very decent civil rights lawyer Mark Darcy (Colin Firth), who had had his marriage wrecked by the lascivious Cleaver. The character redefined Zellweger's star image, bearing testament to her success in the role, but blurring the division between fact and fiction. Over seven years later, her star image is centred on this alter ego, as is manifest in the *Daily Mail* story from 2008: 'Is Renee Zellweger Turning Into Bridget Jones? Weight up and down like a yo-yo. Plagued by insecurities. A tendency to bounce from one bad relationship to another ... Remind you of anyone, Renee?' (Donnelly, 2008).

Her casting caused controversy, as Bridget Jones was a very English character, and so Zellweger was not an obvious choice; yet this created enormous press interest as she underwent a dramatic transformation in order to bring authenticity to the part. She followed in the footsteps of many a great Method actor in undertaking work experience in a British publishing office, undergoing a 'gruelling' diet in order to gain weight, and developing an English accent. The weight gain created the greatest furore as the media dwelt on the personal cost to Zellweger, and have subsequently focused relentlessly on her weight, usually musing on how thin she is, linking it to her supposed 'unhappiness' as a result of being single.

Bridget Jones's Diary displays many of the signature traits of the Working Title romcom, including the idealised representation of London and England for an American audience, an American star, the offbeat, quirky British humour, Hugh Grant, and the mark of Richard Curtis on the screenplay. Nevertheless, the film has a female central character and perspective, the original book and screenplay being written by Helen Fielding, and the film itself is directed by a woman, Sharon Macguire. The book, and the film, met with some criticism for their representation of the central character as a needy, neurotic woman who seemingly can only find happiness and fulfilment through a man, marriage and family. An early scene in the film sees Bridget despondent in her flat, drinking and smoking, fruitlessly checking her answer phone, and then poignantly singing along to the soundtrack 'All By Myself'. Yet she is also represented as a sensual being who enjoys and initiates sex, defining herself through bodily pleasures and excess· rather than cerebral abilities. Cleaver (Grant) is drawn to her because she offers obvious pleasures, with her much dwelt-on short skirts and her giggly crush on him. He is turned on by her big pants, sighing 'Hello Mummy', signifying a quasi-Oedipal desire for her womanly curves.

Kathleen Rowe observes that 'The transgressive, round female body is also the maternal body' (1995: 63), in her exploration of the 'unruly woman' in film. Bridget Jones is 'unruly' in her excess: her curves, consumption, sexual appetite and desires. She is prone to becoming entangled in humiliating situations as a result of her excess, whether it be the out-of-tune, drunken karaoke performance at the office party or dressed as a Playboy bunny at a respectable party. As Mark Darcy observes, 'There are elements of the ridiculous about you, your mother ... and you really are an appallingly bad public speaker, and you tend to let whatever's in your head come out of your mouth without much consideration of the consequences', before declaring his feelings towards her. The narrative validates Bridget's excess and unruliness as she wins the good man in the shape of Darcy, who declares that he

Figure 6.1 *Bridget Jones*: excess and unruliness.

loves her for the way she is, and this becomes her mantra as she realises that she does not need to change in order to find happiness.

The film adaptation of the book constructs Bridget's character as a wayward child lurching from one disaster to the next. She is an only child who has failed to establish a life that is independent of her parents, attending the requisite family parties, humiliated by wearing the outfits her mother chooses for her, and pestered by the lecherous family friend. Zellweger's performance foregrounds her emotional volatility as she struggles to reconcile her instincts with the parameters of adult life. Her curves and exuberance make her very much the child, in contrast to the restraint of Darcy, who fulfils the role of the remote and seemingly disapproving adult.

Stephanie Zacharek (2001) commented that Bridget Jones isn't 'so much a character as a miniskirted confluence of every stock insecurity that single women nearing the end of their baby-making years are alleged to feel'. Zellweger was keen to signal her empathy with the character in the publicity surrounding the film's release, declaring that she could relate to Bridget's tortured pursuit of happiness: 'I'm about to enter the stage of life that Bridget is experiencing and I, like so many people understood her quest' (Brooks, 2001). Yet it was universally noted how quick Zellweger was to lose the weight that she had gained for the role, and subsequently to disassociate herself from this transgressive, unruly woman who is clearly not a conventional Hollywood archetype. Nevertheless, she was unable to evade Bridget's shadow completely, being of a similar age and conspicuously single, after a high-profile relationship with Jim Carey.

Bridget Jones's Diary earned Zellweger an Oscar nomination for Best Actress and established her as a major Hollywood star. She went on to gain impressive reviews for her performance as Roxie Hart in the musical *Chicago*, leading to a second Oscar nomination. Roxie is desperate for fame as a vaudeville star, shooting her lover when she discovers that he has betrayed her ambitions. The role required Zellweger to dance and sing, and plays 'on the audience's affection for Ms. Zellweger's scrappy Kewpie-doll-with-a-heart image before exposing the knowing smirk and steel-jacketed ambition looming beneath Roxie's dimples' (Mitchell, 2002). *Chicago's* period setting and glamour added a new facet to Zellweger's star persona, which she brought to her performance in her next romantic comedy, *Down With Love*.

Down With Love is set in the early 1960s and features stylised performances, elaborate set pieces and mises-en-scène. The film is a pastiche of the Doris Day/Rock Hudson sex comedies, from which it lifts its plot, characters and mise-en-scène. Inevitably, Zellweger's performance is compared to Doris Day; as one reviewer comments, 'she manages, as Ms. Day did, to swivel engagingly between goofiness and sex appeal, and to look her grown-up age even when she is called upon to be utterly childish' (Scott, 2003a). Zellweger's dancing and singing abilities had not been unanimously well received in reviews of *Chicago*, yet are still put to use in the closing title sequence, in an effort to further cultivate the similarities with Day.

Zellweger plays the part of Barbara Novak, who becomes a publishing phenomenon with her book *Down With Love*. The book advocates a proto-feminist stance to relationships, advising women to free themselves from love, have sex without love and replace the need for men with other sources of pleasure, such as chocolate, thereby becoming the equals of men in the workplace and in relationships. Novak is let down repeatedly by the successful magazine journalist and playboy, Catcher Block, in her efforts to publicise her book. Block is snubbed in turn by Novak, as she cites him as an example of the worst kind of man during a television interview. He develops a plan in which he sets out to make Novak fall in love in him, and hence to prove that she is just the same as all other women. The film borrows extensively from the plots of *Pillow Talk* and *Lover Come Back*, with the hero masquerading as another in order to hoodwink the woman into falling in love with him, before being unmasked and having to inveigle his way back into her favour, after inevitably finding that *he* has fallen in love with her. The film concludes with the couple dangling from a helicopter as they are carried away to Las Vegas to be married.

Zellweger's character exudes feistiness and independence in her feminist stance, initially seeming to be the antithesis of Bridget Jones in her attitude to men. Yet her brand of feminism is made far-fetched and ridiculous as she proclaims 'Down with love ... Up with chocolate', undermining any attempt to politicise the gender issues. Essentially, the film is very much of its post-feminist era, with its message of supposed equality; Novak ends the film as a powerful business woman, yet undermines her own campaign in agreeing to forgive and marry Block, despite his clear track record as a habitual philanderer. The conclusion of the film draws on the post-feminist belief in 'having it all', career and marriage – having an ironic resonance, considering Zellweger's own single status. The central female characters pose, pout and preen throughout the film, walking and standing with exaggerated sensuality, making them comical in this seeming excess of femininity. This excess is mirrored in their dress, the colour and shapes of their retro costumes making them simultaneously ridiculous and sensual. These qualities were also central to the physical appeal of Bridget Jones, as accentuated in her fleshy physicality and clinging garments, which are a comic motif in both the films, as highlighted in the slapstick comedy of Jones's humiliation when her backside is filmed from below, as she comes down the pole at the fire station.

Barbara Novak and Bridget Jones are similar in being characters that have been overlooked and abused at the hands of a playboy boss. This is revealed in the twist in the plot when Novak confesses that she was actually one of Block's former secretaries, who had been inspired by her love for him to go to the lengths of writing an international best seller so as to get his attention. Both characters are motivated by a man to take action, although Novak becomes a successful woman in her own right, whereas Jones remains something of a laughing stock in her workplace. Block is an obvious parallel to Daniel Cleaver in his promiscuous nonchalance and his cynical exploitation of women. Zellweger's character again wins her man, although this time he has to come to her to beg her forgiveness. Novak, just like Jones, is integrated into the patriarchy through her union with her erstwhile foe; both

Novak and Jones yearn for marriage and become dangerous in the havoc they create through their excessive desires, which are finally channelled as both of them are ultimately 'rewarded', with marriage, for their suffering and resilience. Down With Love finishes with our heroine seeming to win her man on her terms, having proved her innate ability in her success as an author, role model and business woman. Yet ultimately it seems to be Block's victory as he sweeps Novak away in a romantic gesture, dangling from his helicopter, to the wedding he has already organised, having presumed her consent to his proposal.

Down With Love developed Zellweger's persona as a romantic comedy star, explicitly referencing Doris Day in its homage to her best-known films. On the surface, the character of Barbara seemed to be very different to Bridget's, yet it can be seen as startlingly similar in significant ways. Barbara displays similar character traits to Bridget's, yet within an ironic 1960s mise-en-scène, and the narrative framework of the sex comedy. The film looks and sounds very different to the contemporary romantic comedy that Bridget Jones has defined, with its glamour and retro appeal, yet ultimately serves to reinforce Zellweger's romcom persona as the needy woman who can only find happiness with a man. This neediness stands in contrast to the strong, independent heroines of many romantic comedies, such as Susan Vance in Bringing Up Baby, Jan Morrow in Pillow Talk, and Annie in Annie Hall; it certainly seems to be more typical of the heroine of the contemporary genre cycle.

The film was a critical flop, and did not do well at the box office. Zellweger went on from this to earn an Academy Award for Supporting Actress in Cold Mountain, a Civil War romance, playing the role of the handy country girl Ruby, being something of a departure from her other roles – 'a no-nonsense spitfire … wild-haired and ornery … Her earthiness warms up Cold Mountain considerably' (Scott, 2003b) – yet drawing on the ordinariness which is essential to her persona. Her celebrity status was further fuelled by the press attention engendered by her relationship with Jack White, of The White Stripes, whom she met whilst filming Cold Mountain. The relationship lasted two years, and yet ended amidst rumours that Zellweger was not prepared to forsake her career for settling down with the musician.

Zellweger's eventful personal life was the backdrop to the making of *Bridget Jones: The Edge of Reason*. The sequel sees Bridget breaking up with Darcy as a result of her insecurity and jealousy, and then becoming embroiled with Cleaver whilst filming 'The Smooth Guide' in Thailand. Bridget ends up in a Thai jail, wrongly accused of drug smuggling, and Darcy engineers her release. The film finishes with Bridget and Darcy reconciled and engaged. Bridget is a character who yearns for security and love, yet who struggles to maintain control, both of her insecurities and of her life. She is a victim who has to be rescued by the adult, Darcy, and can only find happiness with a man. One critic commented on how the film conspires to humiliate Bridget throughout, noting that in this case it is a female director (Beeban Kidron) who is responsible: 'If there's a way to make Bridget look *physically* foolish, the filmmakers find it ... Kidron, reminding us that women can be every bit the insensitive dunderheads men can, winds up treating Bridget (and filming Zellweger) as if she really were the pathetic porker she fears herself to be' (Taylor, 2004). It is Bridget's vulnerability that again triumphs, as her neediness is rewarded and Darcy resumes his role as her protector, who is prepared to fight for her honour.

This vulnerability is engrained in Zellweger's star persona, but nevertheless she continues to maintain a reputation for being a dedicated and independent professional, who is committed to her film career to the extent of remoulding her body for a role. Haskell comments on how this contradictory image is typical of 'the most independent minded heroines ... suggest[ing] a vulnerability that is the underside, even the guilt, of self-sufficiency, the vulnerability of women who dare to lay themselves on the line' (Haskell, 1987: 10). Zellweger's romantic comedy roles draw on this tension between independence and vulnerability, yet her role as Bridget Jones has fixed her star image as the hapless single woman whose life is not complete without husband and children. Haskell points out that often stars can become 'frozen' in a role, acting out the 'public's favourite act until the free agent, the unpredictable human being, disappears behind the image' (Haskell, 1987: 10). Zellweger's range of roles shows her desire to be the 'free agent', yet the success of Bridget Jones as a cultural icon who defined the zeitgeist seemed to limit her potential and her star image.

Within six months of the release of Bridget Jones: The Edge of Reason, Zellweger's personal life was again making the headlines, and could almost have been an episode within the film, when she married the country music star Kenny Chesney after a 'whirlwind romance'. The marriage was annulled a matter of months later, amidst much media attention, Zellweger accusing Chesney of 'fraud'. The press highlighted Zellweger's desire for family life, but noted how she was throwing herself into her career in order to get over the heartbreak, starring alongside Russell Crowe in The Cinderella Man and Ewan McGregor in Miss Potter.

Her next romantic comedy was Leatherheads, a homage to the screwball comedies of the 1930s, directed by and starring George Clooney. Leatherheads borrows extensively from films such as It Happened One Night and His Girl Friday, creating a postmodern pastiche of references which complement the period setting. The glamorous costume, slapstick sequences, witty and barbed repartee, and the attractive and charismatic lead characters are some of the many ways in which the film references screwball classics. Leatherheads features Clooney as the captain of a 1920s American football team, whilst Zellweger plays the successful journalist who has been detailed to dig the dirt on their new signing, a First World War hero. A love triangle ensues, Zellweger gets her story and ultimately rides away over the horizon with Clooney on his motorbike.

Zellweger's performance in the film draws on wisecracking, feisty, screwball stars such as Katharine Hepburn, Rosalind Russell and Barbara Stanwyck, who played independently minded women who tend to get their man on their terms. Much as with Down With Love, Zellweger creates a character who is deeply rooted in an earlier cycle of the romantic comedy, referencing a bygone era for a contemporary audience. Clooney claimed that he wrote the part for Zellweger, making reference to the timeless nature of her persona. The character of Lexie Littleton is seemingly a significant departure from the contemporary popular form of the genre, being truer to her 1930s antecedents than a character such as Bridget Jones. She is a career journalist who is in control of her life and has a determination and steeliness that make it clear that she is the match for any man. Lexie and Dodge (Clooney) engage in smart and fast verbal battles, waging a war of the sexes that is fired by their mutual attraction, much as in all the great screwball partnerships. They are thrown into conflict by their opposing interests concerning their new signing, Carter (John Krasinski); Lexie needs to expose him as a fraud in order for her career to progress, whereas Dodge needs his hero status to be maintained for the good of their team.

Unlike Bridget, Lexie does not have a support group of close friends, she is not afraid to stand up to anyone in order to make her point and she is not, seemingly, crippled by vulnerability. In the tradition of a screwball heroine, such as Barbara Stanwyck in The Lady Eve, Lexie is not averse to using her feminine wiles in order to get what she wants, as she attempts to seduce Carter into telling the truth about his supposed heroism. Her character boasts of her 'good legs' and her journalistic prowess, challenging and repeatedly outsmarting the other characters. Lexie commands attention with her upright demeanour and attention-grabbing hats and costumes. She is dressed in reds and russets throughout most of the film, reinforcing her presence as a disruptive yet seductive woman. She habitually intrudes into male spaces whether they be the speakeasy bar, the press box at the football game, or as the only woman in the newspaper office. She smokes, drinks and even casually commandeers Dodge's motorbike, throwing Dodge to the ground.

Lexie is a significant departure for Zellweger in terms of her romantic comedy persona, as she is not the needy heroine. In fact, she is affronted when Dodge suggests marriage to her, declaring 'That's a fine idea! Can't make it in the big, tough man's world so get out! So who should I marry? A farmer, and be a milkmaid?' Their partnership is shown to be one of equals, much in the same vein as with the screwball couples. As they ride away over the horizon their dialogue

Figure 6.2 Lexie is the disruptive screwball heroine in *Leatherheads*.

continues the playful banter that has characterised their relationship, suggesting the adventures they will share in their married life.

Leatherheads was not particularly successful at the box office, recouping $41 million out of the budget of $58 million. The film's nostalgic feel and look seemed to appeal more to an older demographic than most contemporary romantic comedies, with both the central stars having an appeal to a more mature audience. *Leatherheads* has the feel of an independent film, in the style of the Coen Brothers, with its quirky humour and musty colour palette that is redolent of *O Brother Where Art Thou?* (2000). The film can be viewed as a move by Zellweger to reposition her persona as she moves towards 40, perhaps seeking the respectability associated with art house cinema by dusting off and inhabiting the shoes of the great screwball heroines. As with *Down With Love*, there is a sense of ironic knowingness in her performance, and in the film as a whole, as her performance openly references classic performances and actors within the genre.

Zellweger has been compared to a chameleon in how she moves between genres and period roles, and has certainly stood out in comparison to other contemporary romantic comedy actors in the sheer range of her roles, encompassing different stages of the genre's evolution. It is almost as if she is searching for a role which fits best, and that her approach to the genre is an intellectual exercise as she tries on different cycles for size. Zellweger has struggled to move away from the genre-defining Bridget Jones, seeming ill at ease with the role's impact in defining her public image. The sheer success of the film has meant that she continues to be strongly associated with the character, as her personal life continues to elude the happy ending that the romantic comedy demands. Zellweger's star image epitomises a very modern problem as she struggles to balance career and personal life, much of her press coverage suggesting that her unhappy track record regarding relationships is due to her career, whether it be the trauma of the extra weight for Bridget Jones, or not being prepared to sacrifice career in order to settle down. On screen her roles within the genre act out various takes on this dilemma, yet provide a resolution that integrates the heroine into the fabric of society as she settles with the hero, whilst Zellweger's single status remains a central focus of her persona.

As with any star, but perhaps more with women, Zellweger's success has attracted a fair measure of antipathy from the press, as reviews repeatedly denigrate aspects of her appearance. Haskell (1987) argued that this was endemic of a patriarchal society in seeking to reduce and diminish the figure of the successful woman. As Zellweger has met with critical acclaim and continued to have a flourishing film career, reviewers have increasingly fixated on her body – either too plump or too thin, and her face – 'Zellweger, who either has a lemon slice stuck to the roof of her mouth or is, as TV's "Family Guy" once portrayed her, an anteater … ' (Anderson, 2008), often dwelling on 'her squinched-up pout' (Zacharek, 2009). In this respect she is an archetypal romantic comedy heroine, not being beautiful, but rather 'cute' and 'loveable', adjectives that recur in her press coverage. She is safe and easy to relate to, combining the ordinary with the extraordinary.

Haskell (1987: 31) stated that with the greatest female stars of the past:

> Whatever the endings that were forced on [them] the images we retain … are not those of subjugation and humiliation; rather, we

remember their intermediate victories, we retain images of intelligence and personal style and forcefulness.

Zellweger has seemingly attempted to move away from a role such as Bridget Jones, where she is defined by her humiliations, especially in *The Edge Of Reason*, to stronger characters such as Lexie Littleton. Lexie is a homage to an earlier type of romantic comedy heroine, who is defined by her strength, style and intelligence. The dilemma that Zellweger is faced with is that her greatest success at the box office has been in the role of Bridget Jones; she has found it difficult to match this success in roles that are less 'loveable' and 'cute', despite her willingness to extend herself beyond the confines of the Hollywood romcom.

7

HAPPILY EVER AFTER?

THE GENRE PARADOX

The romantic comedy continues to endure a critical mauling despite, or maybe because of, its continued success at the box office. The romantic comedy is thriving in the twenty-first century; Hollywood is fully committed to the genre, as it continues to be a significant presence in the multiplex, proving its worth and popularity with regular box office successes. Yet, paradoxically, commentators and critics continue to bemoan the state of the genre, as each high-profile release is greeted by scathing reviews and feature articles which compare the contemporary romcom to screwball comedies in particular, seeing the latter as a golden age for the genre against which today's films fail to measure up.

Such a response has been in circulation for a number of years, as Zacharek commented in 1999 in response to the latest cycle of the romcom, exemplified by the Ephron films *Sleepless in Seattle* and *You've Got Mail*, as being 'ineffably stupid' and 'drearily predictable'. David Gritten (2003) maintained that the problem with the contemporary romcom lies with the lack of convincing male leads, blaming the 'long shadow of Method acting … hard to square with classic romantic comedy, which calls for deadpan devilry, a barely controlled madness, and a willingness to don a tuxedo and look suave and silly simultaneously'. These articles have come to be increasingly concerned about the representation of gender and the ideologies of the contemporary romcom, criticising the films for being reactionary and for promoting unhealthy role models for today's audiences. Anne Billson summed up the prevailing attitude by pronouncing 'Chick-flicks really suck ... their focus seems to have shrunk down to shopping and weddings ... [the female] characters ... might almost belong to a third gender, a bubble-headed one that emits ear-splitting shrieks, teeters constantly on the verge of hysteria and acts as an indiscriminate mouthpiece for the placement of overpriced tat' (2009: 2). The contemporary romcom has been accused of representing women as needy and superficial, being obsessed with finding 'the one' and marriage to the extent of sacrificing their career for a man. New In Town stars Renee Zellweger as an uptight, successful business woman sent to turn around an underperforming factory in Minnesota, who discovers her human side via tapioca, home baking and handmade valentines, falling in love with the rough-around-the-edges union man whose factory she has been ordered to shut down. The Proposal and The Ugly Truth are similar in their representation of successful career women as damaged and dysfunctional, needing the love of a man to recover their humanity and femininity. Despite the critical mauling these films have received, there is clearly a huge audience for many of them, The Proposal having had the highest opening weekend box office of any Sandra Bullock film and The Ugly Truth having topped the UK box office in its opening weekend. The contemporary romcom offers its audience the image of the woman at the top of her game in the workplace, an image that many aspire towards as women continue to thrive in education, outperforming the boys; but in reality such career success remains a fantasy for many women. The romcom acknowledges the female dilemma around 'having it all', suggesting that true happiness can only be gained through love and that it is something all women can strive for, regardless of status in the workplace. Zacharek (1999) opined that such films are 'flimsy therapy substitutes designed to make women feel good about themselves ... they've become repositories for all the things that women are said to feel most insecure about ... tell[ing] us, "See this woman's a lot more pathetic than you are, and even *she* managed to find a guy!"'

BROMANCE

One particularly successful direction taken by the contemporary romantic comedy has been the male-centred romcom, which moves the narrative away from the female perspective to embrace a more male-centred narrative (see Chapter 3 for more discussion of the 'homme-com'). Films such as *Knocked Up* and *Forgetting Sarah Marshall* have taken the romcom to a male audience, reinvigorating the genre blueprint by borrowing heavily from comedian comedy, employing gross-out humour, reassuringly imperfect leading men and gorgeous women who fall at their feet. The success of this cycle has been exploited further in the emergence of the 'bromance' or 'bromcom'. The bromance centres on the relationship between male characters, following a similar trajectory to the heterosexual relationship that is central to the romcom; examples include *Wedding Crashers*, *Superbad*, *I Love You Man* and *The Hangover*. In *I Love You Man*, LA estate agent Peter (Paul Rudd) sets out to find a best friend to be his best man at his wedding, going through the perils of 'man-dates' before he encounters Sydney (Jason Segal) at an open house in a meet-cute (it transpires that Sydney gate-crashes these events to find rich women, establishing his innate heterosexuality). The couple's relationship develops as they start to see more of each other, talking on the phone, hanging out at Sydney's man-cave, to the extent of Peter's girlfriend being unnerved by their closeness.

The two friends have a falling-out, then realise their errors and how much they mean to each other, before there's a race-against-time climax as Sydney races to Peter's wedding on a frustratingly slow scooter in order to finally honour his commitment to be the best man. The film examines the dynamics of male friendships as Peter and Sydney learn

Figure 7.1 Bromantic love excludes the woman in *I Love You Man*.

from each other and become happier and more fulfilled as a result of their relationship. Phil Powrie observes that this fascination with male friendship 'goes right back to Ancient Greek culture. Here the relationships between men were deemed superior to those between men and women. And that's still very deep-rooted in Western culture' (quoted in Maher, 2009). Indeed, heterosexual relationships are marginalised in these films, being less interesting than the male relationships. Whereas the romantic comedy is often about the rules of romance, with nervous lovers stumbling to unlock the codes of how to conduct a relationship (as in *He's Not That Into You* or *Hitch*), *I Love You Man* deals with the rules of male friendship as Peter and Sydney overcome their anxieties to learn how to be buddies.

The bromance is an ironic take on the romantic comedy, which can appeal to both genders at the box office, reaching out to the male audience that would regard the romantic comedy as a 'chick flick'. These films work to reclaim masculinity for a generation that sees feminism as a historical movement and is familiar with conflicting representations of men in popular culture, ranging from the metrosexual icon of David Beckham to the macho posturings of many hip hop stars. I *Love You Man* is careful to make absolutely clear that its two central characters are not gay, but makes a concerted effort to engage with masculine identity. We see Peter as naturally happier around women, choosing to stay at home and make tantalising refreshments for his fiancée's friends rather than indulge in more masculine rituals. The film suggests that maybe he has become unbalanced, needing to recover his male side, in this case by learning how to play air guitar and hang out with his buddy. Much as with many a classic romantic comedy, the climax endorses the flourishing of a relationship which integrates love, respect and, most importantly, the ability to play, a melding of adult responsibilities and childlike energies.

THE INDIE ROMCOM

'Independent' tends to be seen as being synonymous with more offbeat material, smaller budgets for both production and marketing, lesser known talents in front of and behind the camera, and perhaps less slavish adherence to classical Hollywood style and genre. These are films that take a little more risk, tending to play in art-house cinemas rather than multiplexes, occasionally resulting in a breakthrough hit that may open on fewer screens before being shown more widely. It is debatable whether there is much of an independent film sector in existence, as the Hollywood majors have largely commandeered the most significant players as they become subsidiaries of huge media conglomerates. Nevertheless, there continue to be a significant number of releases beyond the mainstream Hollywood product, from studios such as Fox Searchlight and Lions Gate Films.

For a genre such as romantic comedy, the independent sector can provide opportunities for offering something different, innovating or even subverting the genre. One of the most successful romantic comedies of the 2000s, *My Big Fat Greek Wedding*, was feted as the most successful indie film of all time in 2002, having been made on a budget of

$5 million and grossing $368 million (although half of its production budget came from HBO, a subsidiary of Time Warner). One of the most significant aspects of its independent status was the emphasis on ethnicity, as the writer and star, Nia Vardalos, resisted efforts from prospective producers to change the family in the film from Greek to Italian, and to replace her with a more famous lead (Susman: 2002). The independent sector has seen some influential and successful releases which can lay claim to be romantic comedies, although rarely adhering wholeheartedly to the genre blueprint, the essence of independent being the right to play with all that is mainstream.

In an ironic *Guardian* article, Catherine Shoard sums up the key features of the American indie romcom: 'Weedy leads ... Zooey Deschanel ... Chaste bedroom action ... Smiths worship ... Autobiographical impetus ... Retro junk food ... Hand drawn graphics' (2009: 4), responding to recent releases such as (500) *Days of Summer*, *Gigantic* and *Juno*. *Juno* was the sleeper hit for Fox Searchlight, leading to a rash of offbeat romantic comedies that dress up the genre with a cool indie vibe for a more knowing audience. Typically of an indie film, *Juno* does not stick rigidly to a genre formula: the central character is a pregnant, sassy teenager, the setting is blue-collar suburbia, Juno's (Ellen Page) boyfriend is the geeky, scrawny Bleeker (Michael Cera) who maintains a low-profile presence within the narrative. Juno is shocked to find she is pregnant after having seduced Bleeker; she decides to have the baby adopted and finds a couple to become its parents. Juno befriends the couple, but discovers they are getting divorced just as the baby is due. She decides to go ahead and give the baby to the wife, as she realises that she would be the perfect mother even though she is a single parent; she then gets back together with Bleeker, realising that she loves him. The film challenges Hollywood stereotypes, with positive representations of teenagers and single-parent families within an unorthodox suburban setting. Juno is in control of her life despite the unplanned pregnancy, and is shown to make responsible choices despite her unconventional, feisty exterior. Likewise, Bleeker stands by her, allowing her the space and time she needs, and ultimately she realises how much he means to her, after she has finally dealt with her crisis once Vanessa (Jennifer Garner) has taken the baby. Even though the film ends positively, with Juno and Bleeker together and happy, it is a low-key ending as the camera slowly pulls out whilst the two of them play their guitars together on the front porch. There is a sense of sadness and loss in the wake of the trauma of the adoption, and with Vanessa facing life as a single parent.

The indie romcoms are very much in the spirit of Woody Allen's nervous comedies; wearing their wit and cultural references on their sleeves, they challenge the audience rather than providing the predictable narrative tropes of the mainstream genre. These films focus on the complexity of relationships, questioning the assumptions at the heart of the romantic comedy, specifically regarding love and happiness and shying away from the stereotypes to be found in the genre, particularly regarding gender. (500) *Days of Summer* pays homage to *Annie Hall* in telling the story of an affair that went wrong, starting with the end of the relationship and then tracking back in time to tell the full story, centring the male protagonist and even using split screen. The independent film may be cynical about love, but lives in hope; significantly, (500) *Days* finishes with Tom (Joseph Gordon-Levitt) meeting a new girl, Autumn, after breaking up with Summer, the subtitles indicating a new 'Day 1' in a new relationship for the protagonist who wants to believe in love.

(500) *Days of Summer* paints a harrowing portrait of the suffering that can be incurred in the pursuit of love, as the film juxtaposes imagery of Tom in the euphoria of his new love with his dramatic decline as the relationship dies a death. The majority of the film focuses on Tom trying to work out what's happened in the wake of the break-up, the fractured structure of the film reflecting his confusion as he tries to make sense of it all. In this respect the film is similar to *The Break-Up*, which is another unusual romantic comedy in focusing on the period after a couple have split up. Gary (Vince Vaughan) and Brooke (Jennifer Aniston) agree to separate, but neither of them is prepared to leave their luxurious apartment, resulting in a bitter war of attrition as they

try to stake out their territory. Again, we see the terrible cost of love gone wrong as the characters strive to extract themselves from the wreckage of their relationship. The film defies the optimism of the romantic comedy, as the couple do not reunite, or even find new love, as in (500) Days; yet they do find the way to be reconciled to their fate, and ultimately leave each other, and the apartment, having learned to recognise the need to move on.

DIRECTIONS NOT TAKEN

For the Hollywood romantic comedy, love remains white, with few notable efforts to venture beyond the mainstream in terms of race. One significant exception to this was Will Smith in the title role as Hitch, a date doctor who coaches other men in how to be successful with women. Hitch falls in love with Sara (Eva Mendes), but finds that his professional advice fails to work with her, discovering that ultimately success in love is attained through 'being yourself', and Hitch and Sara end the film together. In an interview with the Birmingham Post (2005) Smith tackled the race question head on, commenting that Eva Mendes was cast because of her Cuban background, as 'There's a sort of accepted myth that if you have two black actors, a male and a female, in the lead of a romantic comedy, that people around the world won't want to see it', going on to add that having a black male and white female would be a problem for US audiences, and that it was a compromise to cast a woman from another ethnic background. Steven Barnes states in the new black magazine (2008) that 'In "Hitch" [Smith] got to have a chaste romance with Eva Mendes by simultaneously helping a geeky white guy get laid. The subconscious message: Smith is sexy, but not a cock-blocker. If you support him, you'll get lucky!'

The same avoidance of black/white romance is notable in Bringing Down The House, starring Queen Latifah as Charlene, a prison escapee who, masquerading as a blonde-haired, blue-eyed lawyer, has started an online relationship with divorcee attorney Peter (Steve Martin). Yet

Queen Latifah's character is that of a feisty, voluptuous and charismatic black woman, referencing her star persona as being streetwise and hip as she introduces the uptight Peter to aspects of black street culture such as hip hop couture and street talk. The film is essentially a culture-clash screwball comedy, as Charlene proceeds to create chaos in Peter's life in her determination to make him clear her name. Charlene ends up moving into Peter's house and helping him manage his children and life, becoming a glorified maid, the favoured role for black female actors in Hollywood films of yore. Ultimately Charlene is paired off with Peter's Jewish best friend, Peter conveniently getting back together with his wife and thus sidestepping the racial hot potato of the white lawyer getting together with the black woman, even though this would be the natural conclusion of the narrative, in light of its fundamental debt to the screwball comedy. Charles Taylor commented on how the film reinforces stereotypes in its crass attempts to create comedy out of ethnic difference: 'The movie appears to have been made for an audience that considers the *idea* of black people terribly exotic ... [it] seems to be aimed at people who want to consider black style in dress or speech or music some sort of passing fad' (2003).

Whereas mixed-race coupling of black and white in the romantic comedy has proved problematic for Hollywood, Jennifer Lopez has managed to build a sustained film career, despite her background as second-generation Latin immigrant. Her career is similar to those of Will Smith and Queen Latifah in that she made her name as a music star before moving into film; all three actors had already accumulated a significant fanbase that perhaps made them a little less of a gamble as Hollywood headliners for an industry that is risk averse, particularly when it comes to race. Linda Mizejewski (2007) observes that 'the women of colour who have starred in this genre ... are light-skinned women with Caucasian features and the bodies of fashion models', reflecting the dominant imagery of beauty in contemporary popular culture, as the romantic comedy articulates 'cultural wishes and fantasies about the bodies of heterosexuality'. Lopez's looks make her a more conventional romcom star than Queen Latifah, who is very much 'the unruly woman' that Kathryn Rowe (1995) sees as being a key figure in many romantic comedies (see Chapter 3). Mizejewski's study of *Bringing Down The House* focuses on how Latifah's unruliness is given a racial twist, as she represents a culture that is 'unruly ... positioned as exotic, sensual, and far more sexualised than the cultures of the white protagonist'. Lopez's persona entails suggestions of exoticism and sensuality, yet is made 'safe' through her conformity to the prototype of Hollywood beauty. Alan Dodd and Martin Fradley, in their study of her star image, point out how her film and musical career manifest 'constant negotiations regarding her ambiguously racially coded ... personae ... While she cultivates a sense of Americanness much of the time'(2009: 195). Her image integrates references to Latin, African-American and white American popular culture; her ethnic identity is made integral to her roles in films. Lopez's position as the underdog/victim is always redeemed and endorsed through marriage with the white guy, in the face of obstacles such as his mother's disapproval (*Monster-in-Law*), social divide (*Maid in Manhattan*) or someone else's husband-to-be (*The Wedding Planner*). For the Lopez character, the American Dream is synonymous with the romantic comedy fantasy: hard work and stoicism pay off as the outsider gets her man, although needing to suffer and be humiliated along the way. Lopez's film persona integrates references to her ethnic status as being 'other' or an outsider, yet her ethnic identity is tailored to suit her role as a Cinderella figure in her films, who is beautiful yet overlooked, hardworking yet deserving, rescued from her drudgery by her all-American white prince.

Outside of mainstream Hollywood there have been some attempts to position the romantic comedy within other ethnicities. Karen Bowdre (2009) identifies the existence of the black romantic comedy, bracketed and effectively marginalised as 'Black film' as a result of a predominantly African-American cast. Films such as *Booty Call* and *Two Can Play That Game* depart from the conventions of romantic comedy, failing to create 'roles where African American characters desire, find and pursue idealised love' (2009: 116), and persisting in perpetuating representations of 'black foolishness and sexual excess' (2009: 115) that echo the reductive racial stereotypes that can be found throughout the history of Hollywood. Gurinder Chadha reaches out to a broad multicultural audience with her romantic comedy/Bollywood musical Bride And Prejudice. Filmed in India, UK and Los Angeles, and made with British funding via the Film Council, the film sets out to combine the perennial appeal of the Jane Austen novel with Bollywood's vast audience power or, as the New York Times puts it, 'multiplex multiculturalism' (Dargis, 2005).

The Hollywood romantic comedy continues to be transfixed by love between white, heterosexual couples, as it has also been reluctant to tackle relationships beyond the heteronormative. The gay best friend is the closest the genre can get to acknowledging homosexuality, although often merely reinforcing certain stereotypes as a comic device. Increasingly, films such as My Best Friend's Wedding, The Next Best Thing, and He's Just Not That Into You (where the Drew Barrymore character appears to have three gay best friends) contrast the angst of the heterosexual romance with a friendship with a gay man that offers supportiveness and fun. Nick and Norah's Infinite Playlist goes one step further and furnishes the male lead, Nick (Michael Cera), with two gay best friends, whose main roles seem to be to assist him in his quest for romance and to provide comic relief. Love Actually originally featured a lesbian love story amongst its many strands, featuring a headmistress and her cancer-affected lover, albeit as a very minor subplot. The story didn't make it to the final cut, having to make way for the more substantial narratives which all explore the trials and tribulations of heterosexual love (it can be found in the deleted scenes on the DVD). Ewan Kirkland, in his study of heterosexuality and the romantic comedy (2009), notes that, 'As suggested by Andy Medhurst's (2005) acerbic re-titling of Curtis' 1994 film Four Surviving Heterosexuals and a Dead Queer, homosexual and lesbian characters do not fare well within a genre almost exclusively geared towards male/female union.' Yet again, in the independent sector, away from mainstream Hollywood, there has been the emergence of the lesbian romantic comedy with the release of films such as Go Fish and Kissing Jessica Stein, which centre on same-sex relationships.

THE YOUTH AUDIENCE

The teen audience continues to be a lucrative market for Hollywood, with the romantic comedy being a significant genre for this demographic, most notably in the form of the high school comedy. Films such as *Clueless* and *10 Things I Hate About You* are examples of this narrative tradition, where the central character has to undergo an intense period of personal growth and self-appraisal before finding the acceptance and happiness they crave, specifically through the commitment of a heterosexual relationship. For this audience the romantic comedy can rejoice in its feel-good ideology, perpetuating the myth of the ideal love and the optimism of the happy ending. Love serves to rescue the isolated teen from their low self-esteem and crises of confidence, catapulting them towards adulthood.

The teen romantic comedy embraces the desire for acceptance and commitment which pervades the teen genre as a whole. *Nick and Norah's Infinite Playlist* targets an older teen audience, building on the offbeat, quirky stylings of *Juno* (even casting the same male lead: Michael Cera). The trajectory of the love story takes place against the backdrop of the New York indie rock club scene, extending its appeal to teen boys as a potential date movie with an indie soundtrack and cameo appearances by various luminaries of the alternative music scene. The backstreets of New York become a playground roamed by carefree teens uninhibited by the adult world, yet who behave in a generally responsible and mature manner as they deal with the minor crises of their evening in the city.

The film displays a very modern consciousness, as Nick (Cera) is the bass player in a 'queercore' band, his gay best friends departing from familiar stereotypes. Nick displays a world-weariness beyond his years, described in the *Time* magazine review as having 'the gift of appearing both wise beyond his years, and not at all happy about it. He seems prematurely 40, so that any teen trauma has the impact of a midlife crisis … ' (Corliss, 2008). The teen romantic comedy increasingly centres on characters such as Juno and Nick who demonstrate a

Figure 7.2 Fairy tale in New York: *Enchanted*.

maturity beyond their years, and a subsequent sense of disillusion and cynicism which hampers them in their attitudes to relationships. This character type can be traced back to the very first teen movies, such as the James Dean character in *Rebel Without A Cause*, but adds a new seriousness to this particular strain of the teen romantic comedy.

The Disney film *Enchanted* recognised the appeal of the romantic comedy formula for a pre-teen audience, melding the iconography and narrative framework of the Disney fairy tale with the modern consciousness of a New York romantic comedy. Fairy tale characters and exuberant animation sequences are given an ironic twist as they are transposed to a contemporary New York setting, creating comedy through the sheer incongruity created through the collision of fairy tale fantasy and urban realities. There is an anarchic veneer to the film as it questions the message of the Disney fairy tale, as Giselle (Amy Adams) discovers that Prince Charming is not for her and actually she prefers a mortal, single-father Robert (Patrick Dempsey). *Enchanted* cheerfully deconstructs the fairy tale, only to repackage it as a romantic comedy in which Giselle finds true love with Robert, and Prince Edward (James

Marsden) finds his own true love with Robert's workmate, who is deliriously transported to a fairy-tale ending with their marriage in the fairy-tale kingdom of Andalasia.

Enchanted is of its era in taking the past, the fairy-tale fantasy for which Disney is best known, and remaking it with liberal interpretation of generic conventions to appeal to new audiences. The film entertains audiences familiar with its genre references with its ironic take on tradition, yet ultimately the genre pleasures of the romantic comedy are still available in the happy-ever-after ending as true love redeems the central characters.

AND FINALLY ...

The critical disdain for the romantic comedy indicates just how significant the genre is; critics and commentators despair at the 'regressive' nature of the representations of relationships and gender to be found there, yet paradoxically the genre continues to thrive. The films offer a portrait of emotional lives that is seductive because of its simplicity, the message that true love is there for all of us, offering a distraction from the emotional complexities of real life. By looking at the wider contexts, both historical and sociological, of the genre over time it can be seen that the genre has continued to be a barometer for the aspirations and values at the heart of society. The romantic comedy has been a particularly resonant genre as it mirrors the seismic social changes that have continued apace since the early twentieth century, specifically the impact of the feminist movement. As Hollywood itself has been predominant within the world of film, so the Hollywood romantic comedy has defined the genre. The dominance of the Hollywood romantic genre has invited competition within indigenous cinemas, as was evident in the rise of the British romantic comedy of the 1990s, which relied heavily on the Hollywood blueprint, even to the extent of borrowing its stars. The independent sector continues to challenge the myths and narratives of the mainstream, the blueprint for the 'anti-romantic comedy' having been established back in 1977 with Allen's *Annie Hall*.

Perhaps it should be borne in mind that the romantic comedy is about evoking laughter, and this is why it is a genre that is readily dismissed by critics. This guide has shown how comedy plays on society's values and insecurities, and how comedy works to engage the audience, yet provides a commentary on our lives. The comedy of the romantic comedy ultimately serves to reassure the spectator as the characters are put through the emotional wringer, providing a safety net where all will come well at the end.

APPENDIX

Table A.1 Romantic comedy timeline

Cultural/historical/political context	Key developments in romantic comedy
1920s	
Women gain voting rights (US: 1920, UK: 1918).	Cecil B. De Mille divorce comedies in 1910s/1920s, antecedents for the screwball comedies of the 1930s.
Concern about rising divorce rate in previous decade.	
Boom time in US: growth of consumer society; expansion of 'women's work'; movement away from moral/sexual straitjacket of pre-war society.	
First talking picture, *The Jazz Singer* (1927).	
Wall Street Crash, leading to the Great Depression (1929).	
1930s	
Mass unemployment; reaction against women's rights and sexual liberation of 1920s.	**Screwball comedies** (1934–early 1940s): characterised by the chaos ensuing from the couple's antagonism, fast-paced dialogue, insults, slapstick and 'screwy dames'. Examples include *It Happened One Night* – judged by many to be the first romcom, and the first screwball comedy, *Bringing Up Baby*; *My Man Godfrey*.
Enforcement of Hay's Code: film industry's efforts at self-censorship regarding morality, in response to the religious right.	
Rise of fascism in Europe; outbreak of Second World War (1939).	

Table A.1 (continued)

Cultural/historical/political context	Key developments in romantic comedy
1940s War leads to greater opportunities for women to gain equality in the workplace and at home. Post-war pressure on women to return to the home; male anxiety about gender roles.	Main themes are battle of the sexes and strong women working in a male world. *His Girl Friday; The Lady Eve; Adam's Rib.*
1950s The Cold War: US anxiety about communist and nuclear threat. Consumer boom: greater wealth and acquisition of consumer luxuries – cars, TVs etc. Woman's place seen very much as in the home, devoted to husband, children and house. Launch of *Playboy* magazine and publication of Kinsey report 'Sexual Behaviour In The Human Female' (1953). Rise of Marilyn Monroe.	**Sex comedy** (late 1950s – early 1960s): emphasis on sex and seduction. *Pillow Talk.*
1960s Sexual revolution – including the introduction of the Pill; explosion of youth culture, challenging values of parents and centred on hedonism and liberal values. Civil rights movement in the US. Emergence of 'second wave of feminism' (late 1960s).	
1970s The 'me decade': the hangover from the 1960s. War in Vietnam ends in 1975. Questioning of beliefs and general uncertainty. Economic decline in wake of oil crisis. Growth in more experimental attitudes regarding relationships, religion etc. Growth in feminist movement and Gay Liberation movement.	**'Nervous' romance**: interrogates love and relationships; shows a lack of confidence in traditional certainties; couple are not always united by the end of the film. *Annie Hall; Manhattan.*

Table A.1 (continued)

Cultural/historical/political context	Key developments in romantic comedy
1980s	
Thatcher and Reagan in power: domination of right-wing conservative politics. Aids 'epidemic'. Berlin Wall comes down: end of the Cold War (1989).	**The 'new' romance**: resurgence of the romantic comedy in the wake of the success of *Working Girl*; *When Harry Met Sally* and *Pretty Woman*; emphasis on return to the traditional romantic comedy.
1990s	
End of Thatcherism. Emergence of the 'new man' and 'lad' culture; girl power. Success of HBO TV series *Sex And The City* (1998–2004) centring on frank discussion of sex and relationships.	Working Title romcom: *Four Weddings and a Funeral*; *Notting Hill*. *Sleepless in Seattle*; *My Best Friend's Wedding*.
2000s	
Bush presidency in US. 9/11 and ensuing wars in Iraq and Afghanistan. Concerns about climate change.	Rise of male-centred romantic comedy and new focus on sex, influenced by gross-out comedy and targeting male and female audiences: *Knocked Up*; *The 40 Year Old Virgin*; *Love Actually*; *Bridget Jones's Diary*.

FILMOGRAPHY

10 Things I Hate About You (Gil Junger, 1999, USA)

20th Century (Howard Hawks, 1934, USA)

27 Dresses (Anne Fletcher, 2008, USA)

The 40 Year Old Virgin (Judd Apatow, 2005, USA)

(500) Days Of Summer (Marc Webb, 2009, USA)

About A Boy (Chris and Paul Weitz, 2002, UK)

Adam's Rib (George Cukor, 1939, USA)

An Unmarried Woman (Paul Mazursky, 1978, USA)

Annie Hall (Woody Allen, 1977, USA)

The Awful Truth (Leo McCarey, 1937, USA)

The Boat That Rocked (Richard Curtis, 2009, UK/USA/Germany/France)

Booty Call (Jeff Pollack, 1997, USA)

The Break-Up (Peyton Reed, 2006, USA)

Bride And Prejudice (Gurinder Chadha, 2004, UK/USA)

Bridget Jones's Diary (Sharon MacGuire, 2001, UK)

Bridget Jones: The Edge of Reason (Beeban Kidron, 2004, UK)

Bringing Down The House (Adam Shankman, 2003, USA)

Bringing Up Baby (Howard Hawks,1938, USA)

Chicago (Rob Marshall, 2002, USA)

Clueless (Amy Heckerling, 1995, USA)

Cold Mountain (Anthony Minghella, 2003, USA)
Definitely, Maybe (Adam Brooks, 2008, UK/USA/France)
Don't Change Your Husband (Cecil B. DeMille, 1919, USA)
Down With Love (Peyton Reed, 2003, USA)
Enchanted (Kevin Lima, 2007, USA)
Eternal Sunshine Of The Spotless Mind (Michel Gondry, 2004, USA)
Failure To Launch (Tom Dey, 2006, USA)
Fool's Gold (Andy Tennant, 2008, USA)
Forgetting Sarah Marshall (Nicholas Stoller, 2008, USA)
Four Christmases (Seth Gordon, 2008, USA)
Four Weddings And A Funeral (Mike Newell, 1994, UK)
Gigantic (Matt Aselton, 2008, USA)
The Girl Can't Help It (Frank Tashlin, 1956, USA)
Go Fish (Rose Troche, 1994, USA)
The Hangover (Todd Phillips, 2009, USA)
Hannah And Her Sisters (Woody Allen, 1986, USA)
He's Just Not That Into You (Ken Kwapis, 2009, USA)
His Girl Friday (Howard Hawks, 1940, USA)
Hitch (Andy Tennant, 2005, USA)
Holiday (George Cukor, 1938, USA)
The Holiday (Nancy Meyers, 2006, USA)
How To Lose A Guy In 10 Days (Donald Petrie, 2003, USA)
I Love You Man (John Hamburg, 2009, USA)
I Was A Male War Bride (Howard Hawks, 1949, USA)
I'm No Angel (Wesley Ruggles, 1933, USA)
It Happened One Night (Frank Capra, 1934, USA)
Jerry Maguire (Cameron Crowe, 1996, USA)
Juno (Jason Reitman, 2007, USA)
Kissing Jessica Stein (Charles Herman-Wermfeld, 2001, USA)
Knocked Up (Judd Apatow, 2007, USA)
The Lady Eve (Preston Sturges, 1941, USA)
Leatherheads (George Clooney, 2008, USA)
Love Actually (Richard Curtis, 2003, UK)
Love And Death (Woody Allen, 1975, USA)

Lover Come Back (Delbert Mann, 1961, USA)

Maid In Manhattan (Wayne Wang, 2002, USA)

Manhattan (Woody Allen, 1979, USA)

Mickey Blue Eyes (Kelly Makin, 1999, USA)

Miss Potter (Chris Noonan, 2006, UK/USA)

Monster-in-Law (Robert Luketic, 2005, USA)

The Moon Is Blue (Otto Preminger, 1953, USA)

My Beautiful Laundrette (Stephen Frears, 1985, UK)

My Best Friend's Wedding (P.J. Hogan, 1997, USA)

My Big Fat Greek Wedding (Joel Zwick, 2002, USA)

My Man Godfrey (Gregory LaCava, 1936, USA)

New In Town (Jonas Elmer, 2009, USA)

The Next Best Thing (John Schlesinger, 2000, USA)

Nick And Norah's Infinite Playlist (Peter Sollett, 2008, USA)

Notting Hill (Roger Michell, 1999, UK)

Old Wives For New (Cecil B. DeMille, 1918, USA)

One Fine Day (Michael Hoffman, 1996, USA)

The Palm Beach Story (Preston Sturges, 1942, USA)

Pat And Mike (George Cukor, 1952, USA)

The Philadelphia Story (George Cukor, 1940, USA)

Pillow Talk (Michael Gordon, 1959, USA)

Pretty Woman (Garry Marshall, 1990, USA)

Pride And Prejudice (Joe Wright, 2005, UK)

The Proposal (Anne Fletcher, 2009, USA)

Run Fat Boy Run (David Schwimmer, 2007, UK)

Send Me No Flowers (Norman Jewison, 1964, USA)

Sense And Sensibility (Ang Lee, 1995, USA/UK)

The Seven Year Itch (Billy Wilder, 1955, USA)

Sex And The City (Michael Patrick King, 2008, USA)

Shaun Of The Dead (Edgar Wright, 2004, UK)

She Done Him Wrong (Lowell Sherman, 1933, USA)

Sleeper (Woody Allen, 1973, USA)

Sleepless In Seattle (Nora Ephron, 1993, USA)

Small Time Crooks (Woody Allen, 2000, USA)

Some Like It Hot (Billy Wilder, 1959, USA)
Starting Over (Alan J. Pakula, 1979, USA)
Superbad (Gregg Mottola, 2007, USA)
The Tall Guy (Mel Smith, 1989, UK)
The Tender Trap (Charles Walters, 1955, USA)
The Thin Man (Frank Capra, 1934, USA)
There's Something About Mary (Farrelly Bros, 1998, USA)
Two Can Play That Game (Mark Brown, 2001, USA)
The Ugly Truth (Robert Luketic, 2009, USA)
Wedding Crashers (David Dobkin, 2005, USA)
The Wedding Date (Clare Kilner, 2005, USA)
The Wedding Planner (Adam Shankman, 2001, USA)
When Harry Met Sally (Rob Reiner, 1989, USA)
Wild Child (Nick Moore, 2008, USA/UK/France)
Wimbledon (Richard Loncraine, 2004, UK/USA)
Woman Of The Year (George Stevens, 1942, USA)
Working Girl (Mike Nichols, 1988, USA)
You've Got Mail (Nora Ephron, 1998, USA)

BIBLIOGRAPHY

Adams, T. (2004) 'New Balls Please', *The Observer* Features section, 26 September 2004: 5.

Anderson, J. (2008) 'Leatherheads', *The Washington Post*, 4 April 2008. Available online at: http://www.washingtonpost.com/gog/movies/leatherheads,1143252/critic-review.html#reviewNum1 (accessed 12 July 2009).

Anon (2009) 'Romantic Comedy Movies At The Box Office', *Box Office Mojo*. Available online at: http://www.boxofficemojo.com/genres/chart/?id=romanticcomedy.htm (accessed 3 October 2009).

Barnes, S. (2008) 'Review: Seven Pounds', *the new black magazine*. Available online at: http://www.thenewblackmagazine.com/view.aspx?index=1759 (accessed 4 September 2009).

Billson, A. (2009) 'Where Are The Meaty Comedy Roles For Women?', *The Guardian*, 20 February 2009: 2.

Bjorkman, S. (2004) *Woody Allen On Woody Allen*, London: Faber and Faber.

Bordwell, D. and Thompson, K. (1994) *Film History: An Introduction*, New York: McGraw-Hill.

Bowdre, K. (2009) 'Romantic Comedies And The Raced Body', in Abbot, S. and Jermyn, D. (eds) *Falling In Love Again: Romantic Comedy In Contemporary Cinema*, London: I. B. Tauris.

Bradshaw, P. (2008) 'Film Review: *Four Christmases*', *The Guardian*, 28 November 2008: 12.

Braudy, S. (2009) 'My Street Treasure – Renee Zellweger', *The Huffington Post*, 27 April 2009. Available online at: http://www.huffingtonpost.com/susan-braudy/my-street-treasure – rene_b_191416.html (accessed 23 August 2009).

Brooks, L. (2001) 'No, I'm Not Bridget Jones. Not Yet', *The Guardian*, 13 April 2001. Available online at: http://www.guardian.co.uk/film/2001/apr/13/awardsandprizes.culture (accessed 1 July 2009).

Cavell, S. (1981) *Pursuits Of Happiness: The Hollywood Comedy Of Remarriage*, Cambridge, MA: Harvard University Press.

Church Gibson, P. (2000) 'Fewer Weddings And More Funerals: Changes In The Heritage Film', in R. Murphy (ed.) *British Cinema Of The 1990s*, London: British Film Institute.

Corliss, R. (2008) '*Nick & Norah's Infinite Playlist*: Enchanted Evening', *Time*, 25 September 2008. Available online at: http://www.time.com/time/magazine/article/0,9171,1844565,00.html (accessed 20 September 2009).

Dargis, M. (2005) 'Mr Darcy And Lalita, Singing And Dancing', *The New York Times*, 11 February 2005. Available online at: http://movies.nytimes.com/2005/02/11/movies/11boll.html (accessed 11 September 2009).

Dodd, A. and Fradley, M. (2009) '"I Believe That If I Haven't Found My Prince Charming Already, That I Will; Or He Will Find Me If He Hasn't Already": Jennifer Lopez, Romantic Comedy And Contemporary Stardom', in Abbot, S. and Jermyn, D. (eds) *Falling In Love Again: Romantic Comedy In Contemporary Cinema*, London: I. B. Tauris.

Donnelly, G. (2008) 'Is Renee Zellweger Turning Into Bridget Jones?', *Mail Online: Femail*, 21 April 2008. Available online at: http://www.dailymail.co.uk/femail/article-1016229/Is-Renee-Zellweger-turning-into-Bridget-Jones.html (accessed 14 June 2009).

Ebert, R. (1996) 'Jerry Maguire', *rogerebert.com*, 13 December 1996. Available online at: http://rogerebert.suntimes.com/apps/pbcs.dll/article?AID=/19961213/REVIEWS/612130301/1023 (accessed 13 June 2009).

Evans, P. (1998) 'Meg Ryan, Megastar', in P.W. Evans and C. Deleyto (eds) *Terms Of Endearment: Hollywood Romantic Comedy Of The 1980s and 1990s*, Edinburgh: Edinburgh University Press.

French, P. (2004) 'Lob, Actually', *The Observer* Features section, 26 September 2004: 9.

Frye, N. (1990) *Anatomy Of Criticism: Four Essays*, Harmondsworth: Penguin.

Glitre, K. (2006) *Hollywood Romantic Comedy: States Of The Union 1934–65*, Manchester: Manchester University Press.

Gritten, D. (2003) 'Why Modern Romance Is Rubbish', *Telegraph.co.uk*, 10 May 2003. Available online at: http://www.telegraph.co.uk/culture/film/3594212/Why-modern-romance-is-rubbish.html (accessed 3 September 2009).

Hanks, R. (2004) 'Wimbledon: Game, Sex And Match', *The Independent*, 21 September 2004. Available online at: http://www.independent.co.uk/arts-entertainment/films/reviews/wimbledon-12a-547411.html (accessed 1 April 2009).

Harvey, J. (1987) *Romantic Comedy In Hollywood, From Lubitsch To Sturges*, New York: Da Capo Press.

Haskell, M. (1987) *From Reverence To Rape:The Treatment Of Women In The Movies*, Chicago: Chicago University Press.

Henderson, B. (1978) 'Romantic Comedy Today: Semi-Tough Or Impossible?', *Film Quarterly*, 31:4, Summer, 11–23.

Hiatt, B. (2007) '*Knocked Up*'s Judd Apatow: How to Turn 40 Year-Old Virgins and Pregnant Ladies into Comedic Gold', *Rolling Stone*, June 2007. Available online at: http://www.rollingstone.com/news/story/14987801/knocked_ups_judd_apatow_how_to_turn_40_yearold_virgins_and_pregnant_ladies_into_comedic_gold (accessed 23 August 2009).

Honigsbaum, M. (2004) 'Lighten Up, Hugh. Fame Can Be Fun', *The Observer* Focus section, 14 November 2004: 17.

Honness Roe, A. (2009) 'A Special Relationship? The Coupling Of Britain And America In Working Title's Romantic Comedies', in S. Abbot and D. Jermyn (eds) *Falling In Love Again: Romantic Comedy Contemporary Cinema*, London and New York: I. B. Tauris.

Iley, C. (1993) 'What Makes Meg A Star?', *The Sunday Times*, 5 September 1993: 6–7.

Jeffers McDonald, T. (2007) *Romantic Comedy: Boy Meets Girl Meets Genre*, London: Wallflower Press.

Jenkins, H. and Karnick, K.B. (1995) *Classical Hollywood Comedy*, New York and London: Routledge.

Jones, A. (2005) 'Where There's A Will … ', Birmingham Post, 23 February 2005. Available online at: http://www.birminghampost.net/news/west-midlands-news/2005/02/23/where-there-s-a-will-65233-15221477/ (accessed 1 September 2009).

Kendall, E. (1990) The Runaway Bride: Hollywood Romantic Comedy Of The 1930s, New York: Anchor Books.

King, G. (2002) Film Comedy, London: Wallflower Press.

Kirkland, E. (2009) 'Romantic Comedy and the Construction of Heterosexuality', Scope, Issue 14, June 2009. Available online at: http://www.scope.nottingham.ac.uk/article.php?issue=9&id=957&section=article&q=fear (accessed 23 July 2009).

Krutnik, F. (1998) 'Love Lies: Romantic Fabrication In Contemporary Romantic Comedy', in P. W. Evans and C. Deleyto (eds) Terms Of Endearment: Hollywood Romantic Comedy Of The 1980s And 1990s, Edinburgh: Edinburgh University Press.

Maher, K. (2009) 'I Love You Man – It's A Guy Thing', Timesonline, 28 March 2009. Available online at: http://entertainment.timesonline.co.uk/tol/arts_and_entertainment/article5986312.ece (accessed 12 September 2009).

Marre, O. (2007) 'Profile: Hugh Grant', The Observer 7 Days section, 29 April 2007: 41.

Maslin, J. (1996) 'Jerry Maguire: The Hotshot Has A Heart', The New York Times, 13 December 1996. Available online at: http://movies.nytimes.com/movie/review?_r=4&res=9803EFDC173EF930A25751C1A960958260&partner=Rotten%20Tomatoes (accessed 13 June 2009).

Mitchell, E. (2002) 'Film Review; "Chicago," Bare Legs And All, Makes It To Film', The New York Times, 27 December 2002. Available online at: http://movies.nytimes.com/movie/review?res=9B0DE0DC113CF934A15751C1A9649C8B63 (accessed 12 June 2009).

Mizejewski, L. (2007) 'Queen Latifah, Unruly Women, And The Bodies Of Romantic Comedy', Genders Online Journal, 46. Available online at: http://www.genders.org/g46/g46_mizejewski.html (accessed 2 February 2009).

Murphy, R. (2000) British Cinema Of The 1990s, London: British Film Institute.

——(2001) The British Cinema Book (2nd edn), London: British Film Institute.

Neale, S. (1992) 'The Big Romance Or Something Wild? Romantic Comedy Today', Screen 33:3 (Autumn): 284–99.

Neale, S. and Krutnik, F. (1990) *Popular Film And Television Comedy*, London: Routledge.

Negra, D. (2006) 'Where The Boys Are: Postfeminism And The New Single Man', *FlowTV*, 4.03. Available online at: http://flowtv.org/?p=223 (accessed 1 July 2009).

Patterson, M. (2009) 'How To Destroy A Career In 10 Films', *The Guardian* Features section, 25 April 2009: 15.

Phillips, P. (1996) 'Genre, Star And Auteur – Critical Approaches To Hollywood Cinema', in J. Nelmes (ed.) *An Introduction To Film Studies*, London: Routledge.

Potter, C. (2002) *I Love You But ... Romance, Comedy And The Movies*, London: Methuen.

Roddick, N. (1995) 'Four Weddings And A Final Reckoning', *Sight And Sound*, January: 15.

Rodrick, S. (2007) 'Judd Apatow's Family Values', *The New York Times Magazine*, 27 May 2007. Available online at: http://www.nytimes.com/2007/05/27/magazine/27apatow-t.html (accessed 26 May 2009).

Rowe, K. (1995) *The Unruly Woman: Gender And The Genres Of Laughter*, Austin: University of Texas Press.

Ryall, T. (1998) 'Genre And Hollywood', in J. Hill and P. Church-Gibson (eds) *The Oxford Guide To Film Studies*, Oxford: Oxford University Press.

Scott, A.O. (2003a) 'Trading Barbs, Like Doris And Rock', *The New York Times*, 9 May 2003. Available online at: http://www.nytimes.com/2003/05/09/movies/09DOWN.html?pagewanted=1 (accessed 13 August 2009).

——(2003b) 'Cold Mountain: Film Reviews; Lovers Striving for a Reunion, With a War in the Way', *The New York Times*, 25 December 2003. Available online at: http://movies.nytimes.com/movie/review?res=9401E7D91F3FF 936A15751C1A9659C8B63 (accessed 3 May 2009).

Setoodeh, R. (2008) 'Sexism And The City', *Newsweek*, 3 June 2008. Available online at: http://www.newsweek.com/id/139889 (accessed 1 June 2009).

Shoard, C. (2009) 'The Guidelines: American Indie Romcom Cliches', *The Guardian* Features section, 13 June 2009: 4.

Solomons, J. and Smith, D. (2004) 'That's Enough, Actually', *The Observer*, News section, 14 November 2004: 3.

Street, S. (1997) *British National Cinema*, London: Routledge.

Susman, G. (2002) 'My Big Fat Greek Wallet', *The Guardian*, Review features, 29 November 2002: 12.

Taylor, C. (2003) 'Bringing Down The House', *salon.com*, 7 March 2003. Available online at: http://dir.salon.com/story/ent/movies/review/2003/03/07/bringing/index.html?CP=IMD&DN = 110 (accessed 10 September 2009).

——(2004) 'Bridget Jones: The Edge of Reason', *salon.com*, 12 November 2004. Available online at: http://dir.salon.com/story/ent/movies/review/2004/11/12/bridget_2/index.html (accessed 1 July 2009).

Thomson, D. (2001) 'Renée Zellweger – An English Rose, From Texas', *The Independent*, 7 April 2001. Available online at: http://www.independent.co.uk/news/people/profiles/reneacutee-zellweger-an-english-rose-from-texas-680549.html (accessed 8 August 2009).

Zacharek, S. (1999) 'Is This As Good As It Gets?', *salon.com*, 9 June 1999. Available online at: http://www.salon.com/ent/feature/1999/06/09/romantic/ (accessed 1 September 2009).

——(2001) 'Bridget Jones's Diary', *salon.com*, 13 April 2001. Available online at: http://dir.salon.com/ent/movies/review/2001/04/13/bridget_jones/index.html (accessed 24 June 2009).

——(2009) 'New In Town', *salon.com*, 30 January 2009. Available online at: http://www.salon.com/ent/movies/review/2009/01/30/new_in_town/index.html (accessed 13 August 2009).

INDEX